GETTING AWAY WITH MURDER:

The True Story of the Emmett Till Case

REVISED AND UPDATED

GETTING AWAY WITH MURDER:

The True Story of the Emmett Till Case

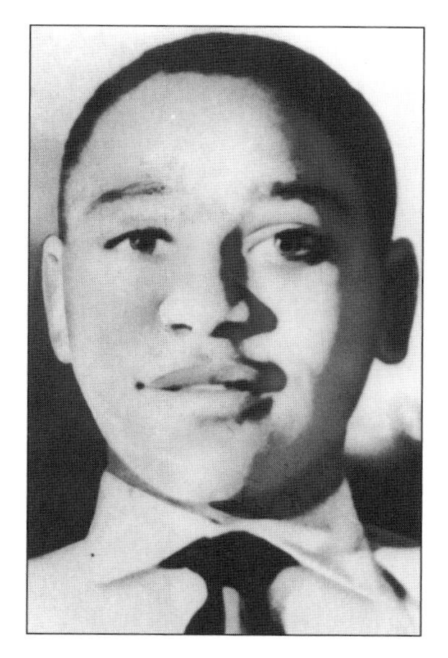

CHRIS CROWE

speak

SPEAK
An imprint of Penguin Random House LLC
375 Hudson Street
New York, New York 10014

First published in the United States of America by Dial Books for Young Readers,
a division of Penguin Young Readers Group, 2003
Revised and updated edition published by Dial Books,
an imprint of Penguin Random House LLC, 2018
Published by Speak, an imprint of Penguin Random House LLC, 2018

Photo Credits
AP/Wide World Photos: pages 34, 46, 53, 109, 115, 120
Bettmann/Getty: pages 19, 30, 33, 38, 45, 59, 61, 65, 73, 87, 93, 105, 113
Franklin McMahon/Getty: page 23
The Chicago Defender: page 67
The Commercial Appeal, Memphis, TN: pages 14, 24, 51, 77, 78, 80, 81, 85, 88, 94, 99, 101, 110, 119
Library of Congress: pages 3, 9, 28 (Dorothea Lange), 42, 121

"New Story On Murder Of Till" reprinted with permission of the Associated Press.

Quotation from *For Us, The Living* © 1967 by Myrlie Evers-Williams and William Peters.
Reprinted by permission of Curtis Brown, Ltd.

THE LIBRARY OF CONGRESS HAS CATALOGED THE DIAL BOOKS EDITION AS FOLLOWS
Crowe, Chris.
Getting away with murder : the True Story of the Emmett Till case / Chris Crowe.
Second edition. | New York, NY : Dial Books, [2018]
Identifiers: LCCN 2017033249 | ISBN 9780803728042 (hardcover)
Subjects: LCSH: Till, Emmett, 1941–1955—Juvenile literature. |
Mississippi—Race relations—Juvenile literature. |
Lynching—Mississippi—History—20th century—Juvenile literature. |
African Americans—Crimes against—Mississippi—History—20th century—Juvenile literature. |
African American teenage boys—Mississippi—Biography—Juvenile literature. |
Racism—Mississippi—History—20th century—Juvenile literature. |
Trials (Murder)—Mississippi—Juvenile literature. |
Classification: LCC F350.N4 C76 2018 | DDC 364.15/2309762—dc23

Speak ISBN 9780451478726
Design by Kimi Weart

Printed in the United States of America

1 3 5 7 9 10 8 6 4 2

Table of Contents

Acknowledgments

Many people have helped me complete this book, and I offer my sincere thanks for their support and cooperation: the student employees at BYU's Interlibrary Loan Office; Emmett Till's mother, Mamie Till Mobley; computer guru Joseph Palmer; researchers Shauna Barnes Belknap, Lisa Hale, Christina Youngberg, and Brooke Anderson; the staffs at the Library of Congress, the Bettman/Getty Photo Archives, AP Images, Time/Life Photo Archives, *The Chicago Defender,* and the BYU English Department. Special thanks to Claude Jones of *The Commercial Appeal* in Memphis for his generous cooperation in providing trial photographs. At Phyllis Fogelman Books, I am grateful to designer Kimi Weart and to associate editor Rebecca Waugh for their help in developing this book. Without the patience, insight, and support of Phyllis Fogelman, this project never would have been finished; I thank her for giving me the opportunity to tell the story of Emmett Till. My thanks also go to Mildred D. Taylor, an awe-inspiring writer, who first sent me in search of Emmett. My good friends Carol Lynch Williams and Jesse Crisler, both of whom are talented writers and readers, provided steady support and feedback throughout this project. My agent, Patricia J. Campbell, gave me the courage to tackle this book and opened just the right doors to get it published. Finally, to my wife, Elizabeth, and my daughters, Carrie and Joanne, thank you for listening to so many awful stories from 1955 and for giving me the kind of feedback and encouragement I so desperately needed. Special thanks to Lauri Hornik for the opportunity to create this revised and updated second edition, to Carrie Crowe and Ella Hughes for their careful reading and feedback on the new chapter, to Herb Boyd, and to Ellen Cormier for her start-to-finish guidance throughout the new edition.

"I have a dream that my four children will one day live in a nation where they will not be judged by the color of their skin but by the content of their character."
—Rev. Martin Luther King Jr., August 28, 1963

I have the same dream for my children and grandchildren and for all young people who live in our land of the free. I dedicate this book to them.

GETTING AWAY WITH MURDER:

The True Story of the Emmett Till Case

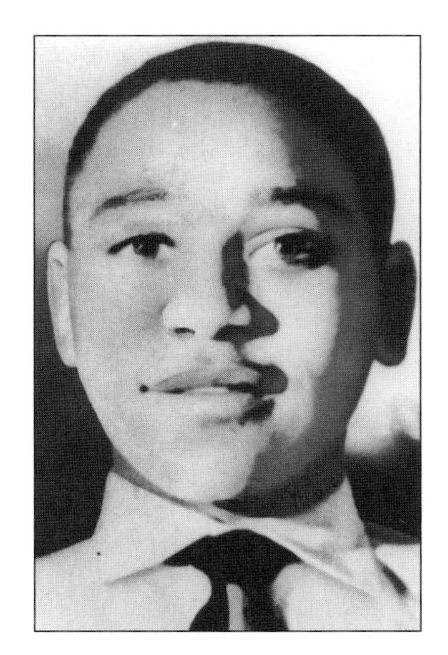

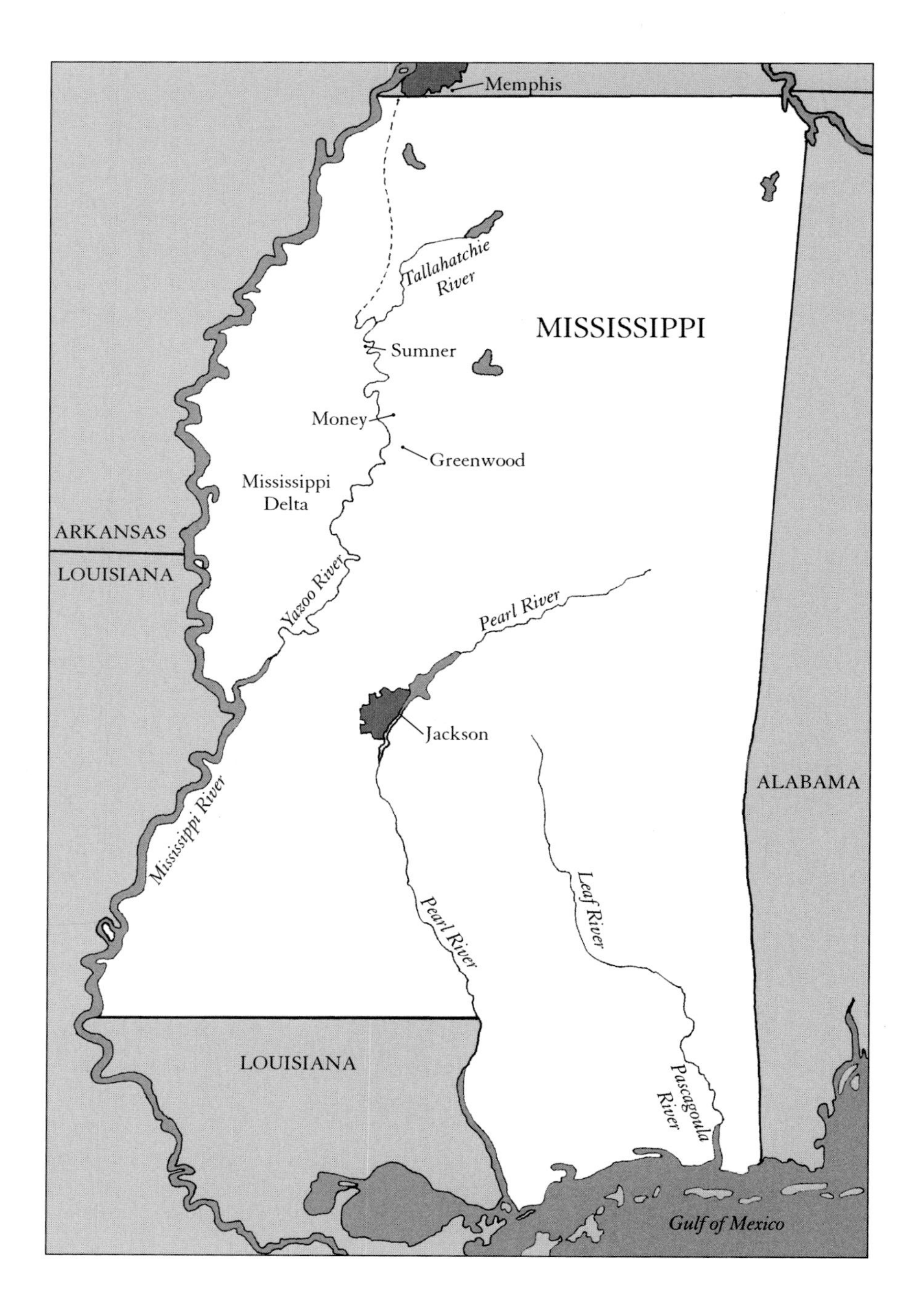
Memphis
Tallahatchie River
MISSISSIPPI
Sumner
Money
Greenwood
Mississippi Delta
ARKANSAS
LOUISIANA
Yazoo River
Pearl River
Jackson
ALABAMA
Mississippi River
Leaf River
Pearl River
LOUISIANA
Pascagoula River
Gulf of Mexico

Introduction

I was born near Chicago, Illinois, in 1954, just one year before fourteen-year-old Emmett Till was murdered in Tallahatchie County, Mississippi. Though his death and the trial of his murderers received national press coverage and especially intense attention in his hometown of Chicago, my parents recall nothing at all of the case or the news coverage of the trial.

But parents can't know everything, so school should have introduced me to this landmark civil rights event; but it didn't. Through elementary school, junior high, high school, college, and graduate school I never once read nor heard anything about Emmett Till. It wasn't until I was writing a book about the life and works of Newbery-winning author Mildred D. Taylor that I first encountered Emmett. In one of her essays, Taylor made a reference to a fourteen-year-old African American boy who had been murdered in her home state of Mississippi in 1955. I followed up on the reference to Emmett just to make sure it wasn't something I should include in my book about Taylor.

What I found stunned me: a gruesome photograph of this boy from Chicago, lying in a casket, his face and head horribly disfigured. The article that accompanied the photo grabbed my interest, not because it had anything to do with Mildred D. Taylor, but because it detailed a critical moment in American civil rights history that I, with all of my years of schooling and reading, had never learned. This article piqued my interest, and I dug some more, eventually finding two very helpful books about the case, Clenora Hudson-Weems's *Emmett Till: The Sacrificial Lamb of the Civil Rights Movement* and Stephen J. Whitfield's *A Death in the Delta: The Story of Emmett Till*. Plater Robinson and his *Soundprint* radio documentary "The Murder of Emmett Till" also provided invaluable background information about the case.

So, who was Emmett Till and why hadn't I learned about him?

My initial research into the case showed that most white Americans had never heard of him, and a review of history textbooks suggested why. In a survey of twenty-one high school U.S. history books published between 1990 and 2002, I found that every book included information about two famous civil rights events: the U.S. Supreme Court ruling *Brown v. Board of Education,* and the Montgomery bus boycott started by Rosa Parks. Sadly, only two books mentioned Emmett Till, and those books used a combined total of fewer than fifty words to describe his place in American history. Neither book suggested that Emmett's murder had been a catalyst for the civil rights movement. A more recent survey of twenty-seven textbooks published between 2005 and 2016 showed that little has changed: three of the books devoted a sentence or two to the Till case, and one featured an entire page. The other twenty-three books made no mention of Emmett Till or of the significance of his murder.

But most African Americans know well his story and its place in history.

In addition to the thousands of people who attended Emmett's three-day viewing and the funeral that followed, hundreds of thousands more, including Mildred D. Taylor, read about his murder and the trial in the African American media of the time. The most sensational coverage of the murder, which included the photo of Emmett's battered body resting in his casket, appeared in *Jet* magazine, and today, many African Americans who were alive at the time mark the moment by recollecting, "I remember when I saw the photo of Emmett Till in *Jet* magazine. . ." similar to the way many mark the moment they heard that President John F. Kennedy had been assassinated.

Emmett's murder in August 1955 and the sham trial that followed it infuriated

African Americans everywhere. For many, the brazen murder of a boy by two white men was the last straw in centuries of racial oppression and abuse. Even before Emmett's death, African American activists had been working to formalize a civil rights movement, but the outrage that followed his death and the acquittal of his murderers finally launched the movement to combat racism in the United States.

To understand and appreciate the modern history of the fight for equal rights for African Americans, American teenagers of all races should know the story of Emmett Till and its impact on American society. This book will, I hope, keep alive the memory of the Emmett Till case and provide a broader understanding of the beginning of the civil rights movement.

In Memoriam
Emmett Louis Till, 1941–1955
"A little nobody who shook up the world."
—Mamie Till Bradley

The first edition of this book appeared in 2003, right at the beginning of renewed interest and attention in the Emmett Till case. In the same year, two other important projects about Emmett Till were also released: Christopher Metress' book *The Murder of Emmett Till: A Documentary Narrative* and Stanley Nelson's PBS documentary *The Murder of Emmett Till.* These marked the beginning of an unprecedented interest in and examination of the Emmett Till case and its place in American history. Using the incredible wealth of information that was not available in 2003, this new edition updates—and corrects—what we know about the Emmett Till case and its impact on civil rights history.

Scene of the kidnapping: the home of Mose Wright, Emmett Till's great-uncle

CHAPTER 1

THE BOY WHO TRIGGERED THE CIVIL RIGHTS MOVEMENT

In August 1955, a group of white men murdered a fourteen-year-old black boy in the Mississippi Delta. News of the murder and the trial that followed it outraged black and sympathetic white Americans across the nation, and reaction to the famous murder case played an important role as a catalyst for the civil rights movement.

This is a true account of the people and events connected to the murder of Emmett Till.

Sunday, August 28, 1955, a few miles outside Money, Mississippi

It was after 2:00 A.M. when the killers' car, its headlights off, coasted to a stop on the gravel road about fifty feet from the darkened sharecropper's house. When the car engine shut down, the steady thrum of locusts resumed, filling the humid night air with a pulsing buzz.

Shadows from the persimmon and cedar trees in the yard cloaked two white men as they emerged from the sedan and spoke to a man and a woman in the backseat. When they finished their brief conversation, Roy Bryant and his half brother, J. W. Milam, walked boldly toward the house with vengeance on their minds. Milam, the bigger of the two, carried a long flashlight in one hand and an Army-issue .45 pistol in the other.

The brothers walked through the screened front porch of the cotton field house and stopped at the door, ready for action.

Bryant pounded on the door.

The house remained silent.

He pounded again and shouted, "Preacher! Preacher, get up and open this door!"

Someone moved inside the darkened house, and soon a voice called out, "Who's that?"

"This is Mr. Bryant, Preacher. From Money."

"All right, sir." The door slowly swung open, and a thin African American man, sixty-four-year-old Mose "Preacher" Wright, stepped out onto the porch.

Milam shined the flashlight into Wright's face and pointed his gun at the old man. "You got two boys from Chicago here?"

"Yessir." He nodded back into the house. "They're sleeping."

Milam stepped closer. "I want the one who done the talkin' in Money. Is he here?"

"Yessir." The old man's voice trembled.

Bryant nodded. "Well, then, we need to talk to him."

With the flashlight casting eerie shadows through the dark house, Wright led the two white men to a back bedroom where fourteen-year-old Emmett "Bobo" Till slept with three of his cousins.

Bryant shook Emmett Till awake while Milam shined the flashlight in the boy's face. When he awoke, Milam asked, "Are you the boy who did the talking?"

"Yeah," replied Emmett.

"Don't say 'yeah' to me," snarled Milam. "I'll blow your head off. Now get up and get your clothes on."

Emmett sat up on the bed and began dressing while his great-uncle, Mose, pleaded for him. "He doesn't have good sense because he was raised up in Chicago. The boy didn't know what he was doing. Don't take him."

By now the commotion had brought Emmett's great-aunt, Elizabeth Wright, into the room, and she begged the white men to leave Emmett alone. "Listen, we'll pay you whatever you want to charge; we'll pay you if you'll release him."

"You'd best get yourself back in that bed of yours, girl," snapped Milam. "Do it now—I want to hear those springs."

With tears in her eyes, Elizabeth Wright left the room.

Emmett continued to dress, oblivious to the danger that was unfolding around him. He reached for his socks and Milam stopped him.

"Just the shoes, boy. We got to hurry."

"I don't wear shoes without socks," said Emmett. His kidnappers cursed him for making them wait while he pulled on his socks and then a pair of canvas shoes with thick crepe soles.

When the boy was dressed, Milam and Bryant pushed him through the house and out to the porch. Mose Wright tried one more time to save his nephew. "Just take him out in the yard and whip him, and I'll be satisfied." But the two men ignored his plea.

Before they stepped into the yard, Milam turned and asked Wright if he recognized them.

"No sir, I don't know you."

"Good, Preacher. How old are you?"

"Sixty-four."

"Well, if you decide later that you do know any of us here tonight, you'll never live to be sixty-five."

"But where are you taking him?" asked Wright.

"Nowhere if he's not the right one," said Milam.

Mose Wright and his wife watched from the porch while the two men walked Emmett to their car. Bryant forced Emmett close to the back window and asked, "Is this the boy?"

"Yes," said the woman from the backseat.

Bryant shoved Emmett into the front seat, sat next to him, and pulled the door closed. Milam got behind the wheel, and the car, its lights still off, moved into the dark, taking the boy from Chicago with them.

*His naked and mutilated body would be found by a fisherman three days later in the Tallahatchie River.**

The kidnapping and murder of Emmett Till and the trial of his killers became one of the biggest news items of 1955. The viewing of his disfigured corpse at Rayner Funeral Home and his funeral at the Roberts Temple of the Church of God in Christ in Chicago attracted more than ten thousand mourners. The grisly open-casket photo of Emmett that appeared in *Jet* magazine horrified and angered hundreds of thousands more. The National Association for the Advancement of Colored People (NAACP), other civil rights organizations, and political leaders expressed outrage at the cold-blooded murder of this boy from Chicago. In an interview, Roy Wilkins, Executive Secretary of the NAACP, labeled the crime a racist act, saying, "It would appear that the state of Mississippi has decided to maintain white supremacy by murdering children." Newspapers across the country, especially those in the Northern states, condemned the killing and the racist attitudes that led to it.

* This re-creation of actual events is based on statements made by those present and documents related to the case: *Look* magazine reporter William Bradford Huie's "The Shocking Story of Approved Killing in Mississippi," *Eyes on the Prize,* trial transcripts, newspaper articles, and other interviews given by people with knowledge of the case.

A huge crowd gathers in front of Roberts Temple of the Church of God in Christ, the site of Emmett Till's funeral

The protests and condemnations from civil rights leaders and Northerners poked an already raw nerve in the South. The white leaders in Southern states like Mississippi that enforced Jim Crow laws, regulations that segregated African Americans from whites, were still stinging from the 1954 Supreme Court decision *Brown v. Board of Education of Topeka,* which declared that racially segregated schools were unconstitutional. In May of 1955, the Supreme Court pushed the issue even further when it ordered that integration of schools must proceed "with all deliberate speed." The two rulings alarmed Southern leaders who feared that the federal government and Northern agitators planned to destroy the Southern way of life. Comments from a speech given by the police commissioner of Montgomery, Alabama, typify the attitude of many white Southerners regarding forced desegregation of public schools:

> "Since the infamous Supreme Court decision rendered in 1954, we in Montgomery and the South have been put to a severe test by those who seek to destroy our time-honored customs.
>
> "Not since Reconstruction have our customs been in such jeopardy. . . . We can, will and must resist outside forces hell-bent on our destruction. . . ."

Despite the Supreme Court's intentions, citizens in the South knew that efforts to change the South would be resisted. A prediction by an editor of the *Jackson Daily News* foreshadowed the violence that would stir up Mississippi, setting the stage for Emmett Till's murder: "Mississippi will not obey the decision. If an effort is made to send Negroes to school with white children, there will be bloodshed. The stains of that bloodshed will be on the Supreme Court steps."

The defensiveness triggered by the desegregation mandate prompted many white Southerners to take offense at the widespread criticism in the media regarding Emmett's murder. Angry editorials like the one published in the September 2, 1955, issue of *The Greenwood Commonwealth* appeared in newspapers in Mississippi and across the South complaining that Southerners were being unfairly criticized for the isolated actions of two men. Even the governor of Mississippi, Hugh White, reacted in the press: "Mississippi deplores such conduct on the part of its citizens and certainly cannot condone it. This is not a lynching. It is straight out murder." By claiming that Emmett's death was not a lynching, the governor hoped to defend his state from the Northern and liberal press that considered the murder a racially motivated crime.

The intense media coverage in the weeks between Emmett's death and the trial of his killers focused worldwide attention on the legal proceedings that would be held in a sleepy little town in the Mississippi Delta, exposing to the world the cruel racial intolerance that existed in the South. Enormous changes in the Southern way of life would soon follow. Thirty years after the case, a former NAACP official said, "I think sometimes that the hand of God was in the whole thing. White men had been killing Black boys down here for years without anybody making much of a fuss. The Emmett Till case became a cog in the wheel of change. Perhaps we have television to thank for that. Television and the printed media turned the spotlight on Mississippi."

The weeklong trial of Milam and Bryant, held in the county courthouse in the small farming community of Sumner, Mississippi, drew a standing room only audience every day, with more than three hundred spectators, most of them white, packed into the courtroom. Newspapers and magazines from all over the United States sent correspondents to cover the trial. In the early days of television, long before satellite broadcasts, the three major television networks even assigned camera crews to report the events of the sensational case; film had to be flown to New York daily. The national and international publicity surprised and angered many local Mississippians, convincing them that they had to defend their Southern way of life against attacks from outsiders. One reporter covering the trial explained the reaction of local citizens to the invasion by the news media this way: "The feeling that [the media spotlight] all was a plot against the South was the most accepted explanation, and when Roy Bryant and J. W. Milam ambled into the court in September 1955, they were armed not only with their wives, baby boys, and cigars, but with the challenge of the Delta whites to the interference to the outside world."

The trial captured the outside world's interest for several reasons. The *Jet* magazine photo of Emmett publicized the gruesome details of the murder, making it more than just another Southern lynching. The nature of the crime itself, a fourteen-year-old boy brutally murdered by two men, made it news, but the reason for the kidnapping and killing—a white woman claimed Emmett had whistled at her and made "ugly remarks"—turned it into big news. The racial context of the case also contributed to its notoriety; at the time, Medgar Evers and the NAACP were fighting hard to gain equal rights for African Americans in the South, and Emmett's senseless murder seemed to symbolize the plight of African Americans in the region. Finally, the murder indictment against Milam and Bryant was a landmark event in Mississippi, a state where more than five hundred lynchings had occurred since 1880, because, as far as many people knew, it was the first time white men had been indicted for killing a black person. The trial gave many African Americans hope that, finally, equal rights for all citizens, regardless of race, might be on the way. For entrenched Southern segregationists, the trial confirmed the fears that had begun with the Supreme Court's *Brown v. Board of Education* ruling: The white-dominated Southern way of life was in jeopardy.

Though everyone involved in the trial already knew the guilt of the defendants, the prosecution, led by District Attorney Gerald Chatham, worked diligently to present a strong case. A number of eyewitnesses testified against the killers, including Emmett's great-uncle. In a spectacularly intense moment, Mose Wright stood at the witness stand, pointed at Milam and Bryant, and stated that they were the ones who had come into his home to kidnap Emmett. Wright's act of courage marked one of the first times an African American accused a white of a crime in a Mississippi court of law. Fearing for his life, he had to leave the state immediately after the trial.

Despite the many testimonies, the clear evidence (including Milam and

A courtroom artist's depiction of Mose Wright testifying against Emmett Till's killers

Bryant's confession to kidnapping), and Chatham's eloquent closing argument, after deliberating for barely an hour, the all-white jury declared the defendants not guilty.

The verdict set off a storm of reactions equal to those before the trial. Segregationists and racists claimed victory for the South. Civil rights activists and Northerners lamented the miscarriage of justice and condemned the acquittal. Both sides agreed on one thing, however: The jury's decision seemed to signal that in the South, Jim Crow laws and racial segregation were not going to go away.

Congressman Charles C. Diggs Jr., center, was among those who attended the trial

But Charles C. Diggs Jr., a black congressman from Michigan who had attended the trial, saw things differently. The landmark trial, he suggested, could be used as a starting point for further change. "The Emmett Till trial is over, but we, as Negroes, should never forget its meaning. The fact that Milam and Bryant were acquitted shows us how tremendous a job we face to bring complete democracy to our entire nation. Negroes and other clear-thinking Americans must combine their efforts to press for freedom and equality through both political and legal challenges."

The aftershocks of the Emmett Till case continued long after the Tallahatchie County jury set Milam and Bryant free. For many people involved in the civil rights movement, the murder of Emmett Till and the acquittal of his murderers was the last straw. If black boys could be killed by white men with no fear of criminal prosecution, something had to be done, and there was no better time than 1955 for the movement to begin.

"The murder of Emmett Till and the trial of the two men accused of murdering him," wrote journalist and historian David Halberstam, "became the first great media event of the civil rights movement." It was the kind of attention that the struggling civil rights movement desperately needed to generate support. With the emotional outrage from the murder and trial, the national and international media attention, and the increased efforts by Americans who were working for equality, the civil rights movement gained the momentum necessary to break free from the social bondage that had enslaved black Americans since before the signing of the Declaration of Independence.

Myrlie Evers-Williams, whose husband, NAACP field director in Mississippi, Medgar Evers, was killed by an assassin in 1963, recognized the essential role the Emmett Till case played in future events in the South. In her 1967 biography of her husband, she placed the case in its proper historical context:

> "[I]t was the murder of this fourteen-year-old out-of-state visitor that touched off the world-wide clamor and cast the glare of a world spotlight on Mississippi's racism. . . . The Till case, in a way, was the story in microcosm of every Negro in Mississippi. For it was the proof that even youth was no defense against the ultimate terror, that lynching was still the final means by which white supremacy would be upheld, that whites could still murder Negroes with impunity, and that the upper- and middle-class white people of the state would uphold such killings through their police and newspapers and courts of law. It was the proof that Mississippi had no intention of changing its ways, that no Negro's life was really safe, and that the federal government was either powerless, as it claimed, or simply unwilling to step in to erase this blot on the nation's reputation for decency and justice. It was the proof, if proof were needed, that there would be no real change in Mississippi until the rest of the country decided that change there must be and then forced it."

On December 1, 1955, less than four months after the trial of Emmett Till's murderers, Rosa Parks refused to give up her seat to a white person on a Montgomery, Alabama, city bus, and her arrest for violating city segregated bus laws led to the famous Montgomery bus boycott, the first highly visible civil rights action led by Martin Luther King Jr. Many historians—and most history textbooks—cite Parks's act of civil disobedience as the beginning of the great civil rights movement, but it was the senseless murder of Emmett Till that galvanized African Americans all over the United States and set the stage for the civil rights movement to begin.

CHAPTER 2

KICKING THE HORNETS' NEST

Emmett Till never planned to be the catalyst for the civil rights movement. As a fourteen-year-old boy, it's likely that he was more interested in sports, girls, and having fun than in the struggles of African Americans for equal treatment.

For Emmett and other African Americans living in Chicago, life was markedly better than it was in the South. Segregation still existed, of course, but the nearly five hundred thousand African Americans in Chicago had many more opportunities and much more freedom than their Southern counterparts. Well-paying jobs were in good supply. Many churches, newspapers, and businesses catered exclusively to black customers. Racial violence was relatively rare. In general, the quality of life—housing, education, employment, entertainment, and social opportunities—was significantly better for African Americans *and* whites in Chicago than it was in most Southern cities.

While it's certain that Emmett knew about segregation—he attended McCosh Elementary School, an all-black school, and lived in a segregated

A young field worker takes a break from her work on a Mississippi Delta plantation

neighborhood—his life in Chicago was a good one. He had many friends, was known and liked by his neighbors, and lived in a comfortable six-room apartment with his mother, Mamie Till Bradley. He may have heard about some of the racist trouble in Mississippi and other Southern states, and in May 1954 probably also learned about the Supreme Court decision that declared school segregation illegal. But these events had little direct impact on him, and as a young teenager who had just finished seventh grade, he probably didn't pay much attention to national politics.

But racist whites in Mississippi and other Southern states *did* pay attention to the Supreme Court's *Brown v. Board of Education* ruling in 1954, and their reactions were swift and angry. U.S. Congressman John Bell Williams of Mississippi immediately labeled the day of the announcement "Black Monday." He accused the Supreme Court of attempting to destroy the Southern way of life and vowed to do whatever he could to resist desegregation. James O. Eastland, U.S. senator from Mississippi, said, "On May 17, 1954, the Constitution of the United States was destroyed because of the Supreme Court's decision. You are not obligated to obey the decisions of any court which are plainly fraudulent." In anticipation of the Supreme Court's decision, some Southern states had already voted to suspend their public education requirement laws in order to avoid using state money to educate African Americans.

Actions to block integration took place outside the government as well. In Indianola, Mississippi, Robert "Tut" Patterson formed the White Citizens' Council, a white-collar version of the Ku Klux Klan, to use political and economic pressure to combat integration in the South. The Council quickly spread to other Southern states. In Greenwood, Mississippi, Judge Tom P. Brady delivered a passionate speech to white segregationists that decried the Supreme

Court's ruling, emphasized the inferiority of the "African race," and predicted the destruction of the South if integration were allowed to happen.

Brady's speech was so popular that in July 1954 he expanded it and published it as a book, *Black Monday: Segregation or Amalgamation . . . America Has Its Choice.* Widely distributed by White Citizens' Councils, Brady's book was read by whites who feared integration, and for them it became an authoritative text they could cite when arguing against the Supreme Court's decision.

Brady's book included a chilling prediction. After a lengthy description of

On the steps of the U.S. Supreme Court, a mother and daughter celebrate the court's decision on school integration

how integration was a Communist/Socialist plot to destroy America and how the mixing of races would ruin our nation, Brady unknowingly foreshadowed the racist rationale for murdering Emmett Till thirteen months before his death:

> "The fulminate which will discharge the blast will be the young negro schoolboy, or veteran, who has no conception of the difference between a mark and a fathom. The supercilious, glib young negro, who has sojourned in Chicago or New York, and who considers the council of his elders archaic, will perform an obscene act, or make an obscene remark, or a vile overture or assault upon some white girl."

This warning from Brady put segregationists in Mississippi on the lookout for smart-talking black boys from Northern cities who would soon come to the South to harass white women and ultimately destroy segregation and the Southern way of life.

Brady also argued that school integration was a Communist-inspired plot that would lead directly to what white supremacists feared most: the end of the separation of the black and white races.

> "You cannot place little white and negro children together in classrooms and not have integration. They will sing together, dance together, eat together, and play together. They will grow up together and the sensitivity of the white children will be dulled. . . . This is the way it has worked out in the North. This is the way the NAACP wants it to work out in the South, and that is what Russia wants."

Many readers believed every word of Brady's inflammatory book and became increasingly worried about the negative effects the *Brown v. Board of Education* decision would have on their lives and their society.

Like *Black Monday*, other speeches, newspaper editorials, public meetings, and books condemning desegregation stirred up fear and hatred in many white Southerners. Convinced that the government was going to destroy their way of life, white supremacists in the South pledged to do everything they could to stop the integration of schools before it began. In an article for the *Saturday Evening Post,* Hodding Carter, editor of a well-known Mississippi newspaper, described the stubborn attitude of the people of Mississippi and the futility of the Supreme Court's efforts to hasten integration: "Ours is a besieged state, but one not inclined to surrender. No one should expect that a decision of a Supreme Court can soon or conclusively change a whole people's thinking." Many white Mississippians felt that their state was under attack by the U.S. government and the NAACP, and they were prepared to defend their segregated society.

On May 31, 1955, almost three months before Emmett Till boarded a train for Money, Mississippi, the political and emotional fireworks that were ignited by the 1954 integration ruling erupted into a volcano of racial hatred and anger in Southern states when the Supreme Court mandated that desegregation of the nation's schools should proceed with "all deliberate speed." Alarmed citizens immediately mobilized—politically, economically, and violently—to prevent their white schools from becoming integrated. Anti-integration protests continued with new intensity, encouraged by the White Citizens' Councils and other racist groups. The Jim Crow laws that prevented African Americans from registering to vote intensified all across the South, making it virtually impossible for black citizens to vote. Some counties had black populations of more than 60 percent, without any black registered voters. Businesses owned by politically

A high school student in Tennessee protests mandatory integration of public schools

City workers in Jackson, Mississippi, paint segregation signs for use in a railroad station

active black Southerners were forced to shut down because banks foreclosed mortgages, wholesalers refused to provide goods, or property owners terminated leases.

Unfortunately, violence against African Americans also increased.

On August 13, 1955, two weeks before Emmett Till was kidnapped, Lamar Smith, a black voter registration activist, was shot and killed in broad daylight on the courthouse lawn in Brookhaven, Mississippi. Though the city square and courthouse lawn were crowded with people when Smith was shot, no witnesses came forward to testify against the killer, and no one was ever convicted of the crime. Other acts of violence and intimidation occurred throughout the South, and many whites considered Smith's murder and other racist crimes justifiable action in their war against forced integration. An editorial in *The Jackson Clarion Ledger* defending the South from the Northern condemnation of the increased violence against black people is a good example of the racist attitudes held by many whites in Mississippi at the time:

> "But just let a couple of Southerners whip a colored person, or let a Negro get himself killed under unusual circumstances and

> every pressure group in the land promptly howls for FBI action, plus rigid laws that would destroy our basic liberties."

Emmett Till knew nothing of the dangerous and tense climate in Mississippi that he and his cousin would enter on August 21, 1955. To make matters worse, as a boy raised in Chicago, he didn't understand anything about the racial attitudes of white Mississippians or the policies and taboos established by Jim Crow laws. Emmett's mother, born and raised in Mississippi, tried her best to prepare him for what he would encounter in her home state.

> "Emmett was born and raised in Chicago, so he didn't know how to be humble to white people. I warned him before he came down here; I told him to be very careful how he spoke and to say 'yes sir' and 'no ma'am' and not to hesitate to humble himself if he had to get down on his knees. . . . I was trying to really pound it into him that Mississippi was not Chicago . . . I explained to Emmett that if he met a white woman, he should step off the street, lower his head, and not look up. And he thought that was the silliest thing he'd ever heard."

Sadly, Emmett Till's lack of experience with Southern customs, his unwillingness to follow his mother's advice, and the brashness and sense of invincibility that many fourteen-year-old boys possess led him to violate one of the South's most fiercely protected taboos at a time when racial tensions were primed to explode.

His cocky and naive indiscretion in Money, Mississippi, on the night of August 24, 1955, inflamed the hatred of two local white men, men who believed every word of Tom P. Brady's *Black Monday* and all the other racist rhetoric that had circulated in Mississippi since the Supreme Court's *Brown v. Board of Education* decision. They'd been waiting for trouble, for a "glib young negro" from Chicago or New York to step out of line. When he did, they made sure to make an example out of him.

An example that no one would ever forget.

CHAPTER 3

THE BOY FROM CHICAGO

Emmett Louis Till lived and died in the middle of the twentieth century, a dynamic period in American history that came after the invention of telephones, industrial assembly lines, and motion pictures but before the development of cellular telephones, DVDs, and personal computers. His brief lifetime spanned a number of large and small events that permanently influenced American life: the Second World War and the first atomic bomb; the Nazi Holocaust and the establishment of Israel as an independent country; the presidential administrations from Franklin D. Roosevelt to Dwight D. Eisenhower; the GI Bill and the baby boom; Elvis Presley and rock and roll; McDonald's and Disneyland; color TV and sitcoms; the polio vaccine and fluoridated toothpaste; integration of Major League Baseball and the beginnings of the civil rights movement. It was a turbulent, progressive era of unprecedented achievements and changes.

Born in Chicago, Illinois, on July 25, 1941, Emmett was the only child of Louis and Mamie Till. Less than five months after his birth, the Japanese attack

Downtown Chicago, 1953

on Pearl Harbor forced the United States into World War II, the war that drew Emmett's father into the army. Shortly before Emmett's fourth birthday, his father, accused of rape and murder of Italian civilians, was executed by order of a U.S. military court. For years, family members, Louis Till's army buddies, and scholars of the case have suspected that the execution may have been racially motivated.

Emmett, nicknamed "Bobo," spent most of his childhood in Argo, Illinois, a suburb about ten miles southwest of Chicago, living with his mother near her extended family, including her grandmother Nancy Jane Carthan. As a five-year-old, Emmett fell victim to the nationwide polio epidemic—polio vaccinations would not be available until 1955, the year of his death—but he recovered without any of the permanent physical disabilities that afflicted thousands of American children in the 1950s. A speech defect that often caused him to stutter was the only lasting effect of the sometimes fatal disease.

When he was twelve, Emmett and his mother moved to an apartment on the South Side of Chicago, where she worked as a civilian procurement officer for the Air Force, earning about $3,900 per year, slightly less than the average income for Americans at the time. He enrolled in the seventh grade at James McCosh Elementary School on South Champlain Avenue and quickly made friends among his classmates. It didn't take long for Emmett and his mother to settle into their new home and neighborhood and to begin to appreciate life in the big city.

In 1954, Chicago had a population of more than three and a half million, making it the nation's second-largest city. Over five hundred thousand of its residents were black, most of whom had arrived in the great migration from Southern states. From 1900 to 1950, African Americans from the South had flocked to Northern cities like Chicago, Detroit, and Philadelphia seeking greater opportunities and better living conditions, and the migration had a significant effect on the size and nature of these cities. The black population of Chicago in 1950, for example, was twelve times larger than it had been just forty years earlier.

Life in the sprawling, windy metropolis on the shore of Lake Michigan wasn't easy, but in nearly all cases, it was better than it had been in Mississippi, Louisiana, Alabama, or Georgia. A major hub of American business and transportation, Chicago had a steady need for workers, and most new residents found jobs quickly. As its African American population grew, businesses sprang up to meet the needs and tastes of the newcomers, offering many forms of employment, education, and entertainment that were not available to African Americans in the South.

In addition to everything else the Windy City offered, Chicago was also a year-round sports city. Fall, winter, spring, or summer, at least one of the city's four major professional sports franchises would be in action: the Chicago Bears of the National Football League, the Chicago Blackhawks of the National Hockey League, and two baseball teams, the Chicago Cubs and the Chicago White Sox.

Emmett loved the White Sox.

The Brooklyn Dodgers' Jackie Robinson had broken Major League Baseball's "color barrier" back in 1947, and now many professional teams employed black players. In the summer of 1954, as Jackie Robinson neared the end of his all-star career with the Dodgers, several other black ballplayers were making their marks in baseball. Willie Mays of the New York Giants won the National League Most Valuable Player Award, future Hall of Famers Ernie Banks and Hank Aaron made their first major-league appearances, and Emmett's favorite player, the White Sox' star Minnie Minoso, enjoyed one of his best years in baseball, hitting .320, knocking in 116 runs, and leading the league in triples.

No doubt Emmett was disappointed that his White Sox finished third in the 1954 American League race, seventeen games behind the first place Cleveland Indians. It's unlikely that Emmett could have afforded to attend many Sox games at Comiskey Park, so he would have listened to the radio play-by-play of Bob Elson on WCFL radio and read the box scores in the *Chicago Tribune* or in the nation's largest black newspaper, *The Chicago Defender*. Like other diehard sports fans, when he wanted in-depth sports coverage, he might have read *The*

Sporting News, the leading source of sports information, or a new magazine, *Sports Illustrated,* which began publishing in 1954.

In addition to following the wins and losses of his White Sox, Emmett enjoyed an active life in his Chicago neighborhood. He had many friends and became known to parents as a benevolent ringleader of the local kids on St. Lawrence Avenue. His friends and cousins remember him as a fun-loving kid who enjoyed pranks and a good laugh. "Emmett loved jokes," said one cousin. "He would pay people to tell him jokes." Others remember that despite his stutter, or perhaps because of it, he sometimes would make wisecracks to people, but his friends knew how to take his comments. In general, Emmett's peers liked him for his sense of humor, his easygoing personality, and his ability to keep the peace among other kids.

In the summers, Emmett and his buddies hung out in the neighborhood or played baseball at Washington Park, with Emmett usually taking the mound as pitcher. His mother regularly drove a car crammed full of Emmett's friends to the park to play baseball. "It's a wonder I never got pulled over by the police," she said. "The inside of the car would be loaded with kids everywhere but in my lap, and some would even ride in the trunk, hanging on to a tin tub that I had filled with ice and pop." Once at the park, she sometimes even got talked into umpiring the boys' games. When the boys finished their play, she'd wait while they helped themselves to a cold drink from the car's trunk and bragged about who'd played best in the game. Then she'd drive them all back home.

Emmett and his mother enjoyed a close relationship, and he worked hard to please her. One day when he was twelve, he said, "Mama, if you can go to work and make the money, I can take care of the home." From that day on, he took over most of the household chores, including the laundry. He used the new Tide detergent in one of his first clothes-washing attempts; the package advertised that the clothes wouldn't need rinsing, so Emmett ran them through a wash cycle and hung them up to dry. "When I came home from work," laughed his mother, "I found all the laundry out on the clothesline, stiff as a board."

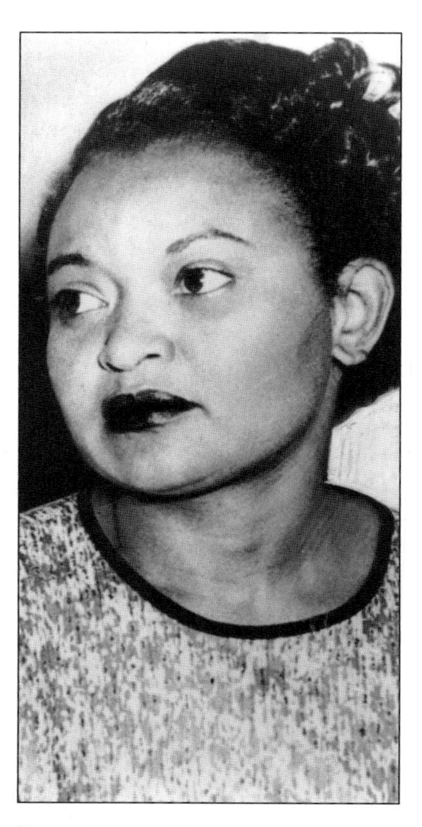

Emmett's mother, Mamie Till Bradley

He once came home with fifteen dollars and handed the money to his mother. When she asked him where he had gotten so much money, he told her he had earned it cleaning a neighbor's apartment. Thinking the neighbor had overpaid her son, she went to the woman's home to see what kind of work Emmett had done and found that he had washed and painted a hallway and cleaned the entire kitchen all by himself. By all accounts, Emmett prided himself on neatness, and it showed in the fastidious way he kept the house and in the attention he paid to his own appearance.

Emmett's helpfulness soon spread outside the home, and on hot, humid summer days, he would haul neighbors' groceries home in his wagon. Some winter afternoons would find him outside braving the icy winds from Lake Michigan, shoveling snow from neighbors' sidewalks and stairways. Summer or winter, Emmett spent most weekends in Argo at his great-grandmother's house, running errands or helping her around the house and in her yard. The visits meant a lot to Emmett and to his great-grandmother, and his mother learned that if she needed it, the best leverage she had to discipline Emmett was to forbid him visiting Argo.

The *Brown v. Board of Education* decision that stirred up so much trouble in the Southern states in May 1954 was hardly noticed by Emmett and his friends. Life in their working-class Chicago neighborhood, though segregated, was pretty good, and the twelve- and thirteen-year-old kids weren't much interested in the politics of the Supreme Court or of the Deep South. Even Emmett's mother didn't appreciate the significance of the Supreme Court's announcement at the time. Of course she was pleased that the United States had made a bold move against segregation, but she didn't expect that ruling would have much direct impact on her and her son. "It was so far from me," she says. "I didn't realize it at the time that the next thing on the scene was going to be Emmett."

The integration order had no immediate impact on their neighborhood, and Emmett began the 1954–55 school year as a thirteen-year-old eighth grader at his all-black school, McCosh. During that school year, his social studies teachers probably discussed the *Brown* decision and speculated about how it might change America, but it was a topic that didn't much interest Emmett. In English class, he may have read some of the brand-new novels that would go on to become classics: William Golding's *Lord of the Flies* and J. R. R. Tolkien's trilogy, The Lord of the Rings. His English teacher might have also devoted special attention to the work of Ernest Hemingway, winner of the 1954 Nobel Prize for Literature. Of course, books weren't always the first thing on a teenager's mind, so if Emmett needed a break from school, he could have watched popular programs like *Lassie, Dragnet,* and *The Lone Ranger* on the new TV set in their living room. If the TV had to be off, he and his friends probably spent time listening to the hottest new songs on the radio, including "Rock Around the Clock," "Maybellene," and "Ain't That a Shame."

In April 1955, Richard J. Daley was elected mayor of Chicago; he would go on to become the first Chicago mayor to be elected to four consecutive terms.

That same month, a new hamburger franchise, the first of its kind, opened in the nearby suburb of Des Plaines. At the time, neither Emmett nor anyone else in Chicago dreamed that the new hamburger joint, McDonald's, would ever amount to much. Emmett and his friends from Chicago's South Side probably didn't even know about the new fast-food hamburger stand in the white suburb. But the big local news that April wasn't the mayoral election or McDonald's; it was the White Sox' blazing start to the 1955 season. By the end of the month, they occupied first place in the American League standings.

On May 31, 1955, Emmett and his classmates at McCosh Elementary were wrapping up their school year, getting ready for eighth-grade graduation, and making summer vacation plans. National politics was the last things on their minds, and the McCosh students probably weren't even aware that in Washington, D.C., the United States Supreme Court issued a follow-up to its landmark desegregation ruling of 1954. Chief Justice Earl Warren inflamed the already broiling racial tensions in the South when he announced that all states had to integrate their schools "with all deliberate speed." To Emmett and most of his friends and family in Chicago at the time, the announcement seemed to have little effect on their lives.

A handsome teenager, stout at 160 pounds and slightly shorter than many of his classmates, Emmett Till graduated from McCosh and looked forward to a summer of fun: He and his mother had planned a trip to Omaha to visit family; Minnie Minoso and the White Sox were playing well; and he had all of June, July, and August before he'd have to go back to school. But Emmett's trip to Omaha got canceled when his great-uncle from Mississippi, Mose Wright, came to Chicago with two of his grandsons. "Emmett heard that Uncle Mose was in town," recalls Emmett's mother, "and two of the boys that he grew up

The first McDonald's franchise opened near Chicago on April 15, 1955

with. They were going back to Mississippi. That's what [Emmett] wanted to do. It messed up our plans completely. After a lot of pressure, my mother and I decided it would be all right to let Emmett go to Mississippi."

Emmett's mother worried about her son traveling to Mississippi, but her uncle assured her that conditions in the South had improved and that Emmett would be safe. Wright had, after all, cleared $250 that year for his sharecropping work, and for the first time he owed nothing to the plantation owner. Life in Mississippi had never been better, Wright said, and he knew that Emmett would enjoy spending time with his cousins down on the farm. Still, Emmett's mother worried that her son wouldn't know how to treat white people in the Jim Crow South and warned him before he left for Chicago: "If you have to

Emmett Till in a photo taken around Christmas 1954, about eight months before his kidnapping and murder

get on your knees and bow when a white person goes past, do it willingly." As a former resident of Mississippi, she knew the penalty that could come with violating a Jim Crow law.

With his mother's permission, Emmett and his cousin Wheeler Parker set up the trip. They'd leave Chicago on Saturday, August 20, a few weeks after Emmett's fourteenth birthday, and travel by train to Money, Mississippi, the tiny country town near Mose Wright's farm. Emmett agreed to meet Wheeler and Mose at the Central Street station for the trip to Mississippi, but on the appointed day, he got to the station late and missed the train. He would never have made it to Money that summer if he hadn't caught up with the Illinois Central at the Englewood station, several miles away from Central Street, just before the train pulled out. Out of breath and excited, Emmett found Wheeler on the train, and the cousins settled into their seats for the long ride to Mississippi.

Money was a tiny rural community on the eastern edge of the Mississippi Delta. The dusty hamlet, population fifty-five, wedged between the railroad tracks and Old Money Road, had never lived up to its name. Its main reason for existence was its cotton gin, a large corrugated metal building that housed the equipment used to process harvested cotton. Over time, a handful of businesses—three stores, including Bryant's Grocery & Meat Market, and a gas station—came to town, setting up on the west side of Old Money Road, just south of the cotton gin. Across the road and behind the train tracks was the elementary school. A few homes were scattered along gravel side roads that branched off Old Money Road and divided cotton fields, and farther away from the "town" of Money, sharecroppers' shacks dotted the edges of farm roads.

Money was nothing like Chicago: It had no city parks or baseball fields, no movie theaters or dance halls, no restaurants or department stores. The air in that part of the Delta hung heavy with sweltering humidity, only occasionally stirred up by weak breezes, and the steady buzz of locusts seemed to magnify the stifling Mississippi heat. Most black people worked in the fields and lived in beat-up cabins owned by white landowners. The state of Mississippi had the lowest per capita income in the nation, and, ironically enough, the people in "Money" were among the poorest in the state. Mississippi's racism was perhaps the greatest difference from Chicago, and the white people in and around Money vigilantly enforced Jim Crow segregation laws. Just a few weeks before Emmett's arrival in Money, a black teenage girl had been flogged for "crowding" a white woman in a store.

From the moment Emmett and his cousin arrived on Sunday, August 21, the visitors from Chicago brought excitement to the sleepy little town. Emmett's Southern cousins and their friends marveled at the ways the Northern boys dressed and acted, and at the stories they told about life in the North. One of the local boys, John Milton Wesley, lived near Money and was seven years old when Emmett arrived in 1955.

He remembers that Emmett Till was different from the rest of the Chicago boys. He seemed more mature, and he talked a lot, keeping Wesley and his Mississippi friends "spellbound with stories of white girlfriends, the forbidden fruit." Emmett wore a straw hat and had "funny-looking, light colored eyes" that the local girls found attractive, but it was the stories of life up North that got the most attention from the kids in Money. Wesley said that Emmett and his friends from Chicago "relished their ability to dazzle us with their lack of fear of white people. It never occurred to us at the time that they always made these boasts when there were no white folks around to challenge them."

The local kids made an eager and gullible audience. Poverty and racial segregation dominated their lives, so the kind of life the Chicago boys talked about seemed as foreign and incredible as the land of Oz. Lacking the sophistication of their more worldly and better-educated friends from Illinois, the Mississippi boys believed every story they heard, no matter how wild it seemed. The children of poor sharecroppers imagined that anything might be possible in the wonderful world up North.

One of the things that impressed Wesley and his friends most were the photos of white women, cut out of magazines, that the boys from Chicago carried in their wallets. The Mississippi boys believed the photos were real and that in the North, black boys could have white girlfriends without any trouble. A society without racial boundaries was almost impossible for them to comprehend. Wesley said, "We imagined racial bliss and integrated movies where blacks didn't have to sit in the balcony. . . . We could only marvel at what we imagined their lives must be like in a place where your seat on the bus was determined not by the color of your skin but by the availability of a vacant seat."

For his first few days in Money, Emmett had a great time. His cocky personality and fantastic stories about life in Chicago made him a local celebrity among the Mississippi kids, and his Southern vacation was even more fun than he had expected.

But the fun came to an abrupt end on Wednesday night, August 24, when Emmett crossed a Jim Crow boundary he never really understood.

CHAPTER 4

THE WOLF WHISTLE

On Wednesday night, Emmett and his cousins attended a church meeting where Mose Wright was preaching. Sitting in a stuffy country church with no air-conditioning on a hot, humid August night made the teenage boys restless, so, early in the sermon, they snuck out of the church, hopped into Wright's 1941 Ford, and drove to Money to check out the action there.

For the poor children of sharecropping families, the center of social activity in Money was Bryant's Grocery & Meat Market, a small white-owned store on Old Money Road that catered to local black sharecroppers and field workers. People young and old hung out on the store's front porch playing checkers, listening to music, and swapping stories. When they got thirsty or needed a snack, they could go inside and buy a cold RC cola or some penny candy. That night, Carolyn Bryant, a twenty-one-year-old mother of two young boys, worked behind the counter alone. Her husband, Roy, was on the road, hauling a load of shrimp from New Orleans to Brownsville, Texas.

When Emmett and his cousins arrived around 7:30, a small group of people had already gathered at Bryant's Market, and before long, Emmett was the center of attention, telling stories about life in Chicago. At one point, he pulled out his wallet and started showing off some of the photos he had with him, suggesting that a white girl in one photo was a friend of his. His bragging drew a big reaction from the local crowd, and one of the boys pointed at the store and challenged Emmett: "You talkin' mighty big, Bo. There's a pretty little white woman in there in the sto'. Since you Chicago cats know so much about white girls, let's see you go in there and get a date with her."

The kids from around Money knew that Carolyn Bryant had won a couple

The flashpoint of the Emmett Till case: Bryant's Grocery & Meat Market, Money, Mississippi

of local beauty contests, making her one of the best-known young white women in the area. All the Mississippi boys knew the risks of talking to her or even looking her in the eye. Asking her on a date would be unimaginable!

The mixing of races, especially a black man with a white woman, was the strongest and most fiercely enforced Jim Crow taboo. The local boys had all heard stories of black men getting beaten or killed for being too friendly with a white woman. Even an innocent glance could be taken the wrong way, and a white woman's accusation of being "molested" by a black man or boy would be all the evidence local white men needed to use violence to "teach the boy a lesson."

Because he had been raised in the North, Emmett didn't appreciate the seriousness of this Southern taboo, and at the time, standing there goofing off with his friends on that store's front porch, he either forgot or ignored the warnings his mother had given him before he left Chicago.

Unwilling to back down from his friends' dare, Emmett walked into the store to buy some candy while his cousins and friends crowded against the storefront windows to see what would happen. No one could hear what Emmett and Carolyn Bryant might have said to each other, and what actually happened inside was known only to Emmett and Mrs. Bryant. Unfortunately, Emmett left no testimony, so the only accounts available are those of the young people who were at Bryant's store that evening and the courtroom testimony of Carolyn Bryant.

It should be noted that after more than sixty years of determined silence about the case, Carolyn Bryant finally confessed that her testimony in the trial contained lies and exaggerations, an outrageous story created by the defense lawyers and some of her relatives.

In the murder trial of her husband and his half brother about a month after

Carolyn Bryant, the twenty-one-year-old "crossroads Marilyn Monroe," who accused Emmett Till of whistling at her

the incident at the store, Carolyn Bryant reported her version of what happened. She told the judge that on the evening of August 24, she was working behind the counter when a black male she hadn't seen before, one who spoke with a "Northern brogue," entered and approached the counter. No one else was in the store at the time. At five feet six inches and 160 pounds, the boy was taller and heavier than the slender, five two Mrs. Bryant, but she didn't feel threatened at first. According to Mrs. Bryant, the boy asked for some candy, and when she held out her hand for his money, she said he grabbed it, pulled her toward him, and said, "How about a date, baby?"

Carolyn Bryant said his audacious question shocked and angered her, and she jerked her hand free and headed to the apartment in the back of the store where Juanita Milam, her sister-in-law, was. Before she made it to the apartment door, the boy stepped in front of her, put his hands on her waist, and said, "You needn't be afraid of me, baby. I've been with white women before."

At that point, one of the boy's friends rushed into the store, grabbed him, and pushed him out the front door. Mrs. Bryant told the judge that before the boys were out of the store, the Northern boy turned and said, "Bye, baby," to her. Furious at the boy's rudeness, she then ran out the front door to get a pistol from her sister-in-law's car. When the boy saw her outside, she said he whistled at her, the two-note "wolf whistle," before his friends pushed him into their car and drove away.

Mrs. Bryant immediately went back into the store and told Juanita what had happened. In court, Carolyn Bryant said that although the rude and uppity behavior of the black boy scared and angered her and her sister-in-law, they decided not to say anything about the incident to their husbands. They both knew that if their menfolk heard about what had happened, there would be big trouble.

The eyewitness accounts from the young people who were outside the store cannot, of course, provide any information about what Emmett said inside, but they can describe what happened when he came out. Some of Emmett's cousins were there that evening and have spoken about what happened at Bryant's Grocery & Meat Market on the night of August 24, 1955. None of them claimed that Emmett had in any way put his hands on Carolyn Bryant.

Various witnesses confirm that evening's events. Most also add that when Emmett left the store, he whistled at Carolyn Bryant. Emmett Till's mother, Mamie Till Bradley, heard those reports, but she didn't believe that her son would have been foolish or bold enough to whistle at a white woman. A few weeks after his death, she explained that what had sounded like a wolf whistle was probably just Emmett's attempt to whistle out a sound to clear his stutter. In an interview many years later, Mrs. Bradley said that the boys who had been at the store told her that when Emmett came out of Bryant's, he was asked, "How did you like the lady in the store?" He reportedly whistled his approval to the boys, not at Mrs. Bryant.

With the lack of recorded testimony from anyone other than Carolyn Bryant and with the various accounts of what came to be known as the "wolf whistle" incident, it's impossible to know exactly what was said and done in a small country store more than sixty years ago, but evidence suggests that Emmett Till did say "Bye, baby" and whistle while at Bryant's Grocery & Meat Market.

As the boys sped away from the scene in Wright's car, they were giddy with excitement about what their "crazy" cousin had just done and about their close call with being shot at by Carolyn Bryant. When they were a safe distance from the store, however, they began to realize the seriousness of what had happened. They knew the chances were good that even if Mrs. Bryant or her family didn't find a way to punish Emmett, Uncle Mose would punish him—and maybe his cousins too—when he found out about Emmett being disrespectful. Recalling that drive back to the church, Wheeler Parker said, "Emmett begged us, he said, 'Don't tell [Uncle Mose]. I don't want you to tell him.' So we decided we wouldn't tell him. There was a girl there, and she said, 'You're going to hear some more about this. I know those type of people; you're going to hear some more.'" But they heard nothing threatening from the Bryants or other whites that night or Thursday or Friday, so Emmett and his cousins assumed the incident had been forgotten.

They couldn't have been more wrong. Nothing like this had ever happened in the sleepy little farm town, and talk about what Emmett had done at Bryant's store blew through the county like a dust storm. Black residents who heard about the "wolf whistle" at Bryant's store could talk of little else, and within two days nearly everyone in the county—black and white—knew the sensational news. Most people could hardly believe that anyone would be brave or crazy or stupid enough to do what people were saying Emmett Till had done. Mose Wright and his wife, Elizabeth, learned about the incident the day after it happened, and fearing the worst, considered sending Emmett home on the next available train; however, when two days passed without threat of reprisal, they too assumed that the incident had been forgotten.

But what had taken place at Bryant's Grocery & Meat Market that Wednesday night hadn't been forgotten at all. A long fuse had been lit, and it would smolder for three days before it finally ignited an explosive and violent reaction that would focus the attention of the entire nation on a fourteen-year-old boy from Chicago and a rural county in the Mississippi Delta.

Around 4:00 A.M. on Friday, twenty-four-year-old ex-paratrooper Roy Bryant returned home from his trip to Texas. He went straight to bed and slept for several hours before going to work at his store later that afternoon. Soon after he arrived, a black customer told him about the lurid "talk" that was going around Money and the nearby plantations regarding his wife and a boy from Chicago.

This news of the "talk at the store" infuriated Bryant. As a racist white Southerner, he expected black people to know their Jim Crow place, especially when it came to white women. Bryant immediately confronted his wife with what he had heard; she admitted that the rumor was true and begged him to forget about it. But Bryant could not forget it. His own fury and the racist code of the South dictated swift and strong action to defend his wife's honor. Even Money's black citizens who had heard about the incident wondered why Bryant hadn't dealt with the boy from up North already. Everyone who had heard about the encounter between Emmett Till and Carolyn Bryant expected some sort of retaliation against Emmett—a whipping, at the very least.

Nothing had happened, of course, because Roy Bryant had been out of town, but now that he was back and knew about the "molestation" of his wife, he believed he had to do something about the uppity boy from Chicago. He found out that Emmett was staying with Mose Wright in a sharecropper's house out on G. C. Frederick's place, about three miles from Money. Bryant had no car of his own, so he had to wait until Saturday night, when his thirty-six-year-old half brother, J. W. "Big" Milam, came to the store. Bryant told Milam what had happened and asked to borrow Milam's car. Milam offered not only to lend his car but to ride out to Wright's house with Bryant to help him work the boy over. After agreeing to meet later that night, Milam went home, filled his car with gas, and packed his pistol and a flashlight for the night's dirty work. He drove back to Money around 2:00 A.M. to pick up Bryant.

That same Saturday night, Emmett, Curtis, and Wheeler drove to Greenwood, the largest city in the county, to party at a juke joint. They didn't return to Mose Wright's home until well after midnight. Exhausted from a long day and a late night out, the boys went to bed in one of the back bedrooms and quickly fell asleep.

What happened next was reported by Mose Wright in a television interview shortly after the trial:

"Sunday morning about two-thirty, someone called at the door. And I said 'Who is it' and he said 'This is Mr. Bryant. I want to talk with you and the boy.' And when I opened the door, there was a man standing with a pistol in one hand and a flashlight in the other hand."

Wright's wife, Elizabeth, knew trouble had come knocking. "When I heard the men at the door," she said, "I ran to Emmett's room and tried to wake him and take him out of the back door into the cotton fields. But they were already in the front door before I could shake him awake."

The two men forced Wright to lead them into the back bedroom where Emmett was sleeping. They woke him, made sure he was the boy "who done the talkin' at Money," and, after letting him get dressed, took him outside to their car.

"They marched him to the car," Wright told reporters, "and they asked [someone] there, 'Was this the right boy?' and the answer was, 'It is.'" Bryant and Milam then pushed Emmett into the car and drove off.

That was the last time Mose Wright saw Emmett Till alive.

Only two sources contain details of what happened after the men left Wright's home: murder trial transcripts, which disappeared a few years after the trial, and the post-trial interviews Bryant and Milam had with journalist William Bradford Huie. Portions of the courtroom testimony can still be found in archives of local and national newspapers that covered the trial and in Hugh Stephen Whittaker's 1963 master's thesis about the Emmett Till murder. Excerpts from the Huie interviews appeared in *Look* magazine and *Reader's*

Emmett Till's great-uncle, Mose Wright, outside the Tallahatchie County courthouse waiting to testify in the case

Digest; Huie published a full account in his book *Wolf Whistle and Other Stories*. Because the killers may have been protecting others involved in the kidnapping and murder, their version of the story cannot be assumed to be completely accurate. The following account is based on information from all these sources; where the sources don't agree, the trial testimony takes precedence over the information from Huie's interviews.

After leaving Wright's home, the men dropped off the woman who had been in the car, probably Carolyn Bryant, and drove around Tallahatchie County hoping to scare and intimidate Emmett. At dawn on Sunday, they drove to a shed on the plantation owned by one of Milam's brothers. Willie Reed, the son of a sharecropper, testified in court that he saw Emmett sitting in the back of a pickup truck carrying two other African Americans and four white men, one of whom Reed identified as J. W. Milam. Reed said that later that morning he heard sounds of a beating and cries of "Mama, Lord have mercy. Lord have mercy!" coming from inside the shed, and saw Milam, carrying a pistol, leave the shed to draw water from a well. Three other white men were with him.

After the cries stopped, Reed watched as a truck backed up to the shed and three African American men helped the white men load something wrapped in a tarp into the truck. Later that day he saw the black workers hosing blood out of the pickup's bed.

It's not known if Emmett was dead or alive when they left the shed. According to Bryant and Milam, after beating Emmett, they took him to the Tallahatchie River and ordered him to strip. Milam claimed that even after the beatings, Emmett showed no remorse for what he had done at Bryant's Market. That's when Milam "decided it was time a few people got put on notice," and he made up his mind to kill Emmett, "just so everybody could know how me and my folks stand." When their evil deed was finished, Bryant, Milam, and whoever

J. W. Milam, left, and Roy Bryant accompanied by Sheriff H. C. Strider on their way to the trial

else was involved returned to the plantation, burned Emmett's clothes and shoes, and then went home to bed.

Back at Mose Wright's home, Emmett's relatives could hardly believe what had happened that night and were frantic with worry about Emmett. "When I woke up the next morning," said Curtis Jones, one of Emmett's cousins, "I thought it was a dream. I went to the porch and my grandfather was sitting on the porch. I asked him, 'Poppa, did they bring Bo back?' He said, 'No.' He said, 'I hope they didn't kill that boy.'

"I asked him, 'Ain't you going to call the police?' He said, 'No, I can't call the police. They told me that if I call the sheriff, they was going to kill everybody in this house.' So I told him, I say, 'I'll call.' That happened Sunday."

Using a neighbor's phone, Curtis called George W. Smith, the Leflore County sheriff, to report the kidnapping. Then he called his mother, Willie Mae Jones, in Chicago to tell her what had happened. Jones immediately called Emmett's mother, Mamie Till Bradley.

Mrs. Jones was hysterical on the phone, and at first Mrs. Bradley couldn't understand what she was so upset about. When she finally heard clearly what had happened in Mississippi, Mrs. Bradley knew her son was in serious danger, but from her home in Chicago, she could do little except stay in contact with Mississippi relatives for news about Emmett. She also called Chicago police and asked them to pressure Mississippi authorities to look into the disappearance of Emmett Till.

"I did two things that were unexpected," Mrs. Bradley told an audience in 1999. "I made up my bed, and I began calling every newspaper I could think of . . . I had expected no response from the newspapers, but to my surprise, everyone I called responded instantly.

"It was just amazing. I think the papers and the television and the radio, it seemed like they just latched on. And when they latched on, they would just not let go."

The phone calls worked. Around 2:00 Sunday afternoon, Sheriff Smith drove from Greenwood to Money and arrested Roy Bryant for kidnapping. Later that day, J. W. Milam was picked up and he joined Bryant in the Leflore County jail on the same charges. Both men admitted they had kidnapped Emmett from his uncle's home, but, they told the sheriff, they turned him loose after they took him to Bryant's store for identification and Carolyn Bryant said he wasn't the man who had harassed her.

Bryant and Milam remained in jail while Sheriff Smith and Tallahatchie County Sheriff H. C. Strider searched for a third man involved in the kidnapping and gathered evidence to build a case against the suspects already in custody. In the days immediately after the arrests, neither the sheriffs nor Emmett's relatives could find any trace of the missing boy.

Wednesday morning, August 31, three days after the arrest of Bryant and Milam, a seventeen-year-old white boy, Robert Hodges, fishing on the Tallahatchie River saw a pair of knees sticking out of shallow water. Not sure what he had found, Hodges contacted the Tallahatchie County sheriff's office, and soon deputies arrived on the scene to retrieve the body. They brought Mose Wright to the river with them to identify the badly mutilated and decomposed corpse.

The body had swollen to almost twice its normal size; the head had been severely beaten, "torture, horrible beating," said one deputy. One side of the victim's forehead was crushed, an eye had been gouged out, and the skull had a bullet hole just above the right ear. The neck had been ripped raw by the barbed wire wrapped around it. The beatings and three days in the river had turned the face and head into a monstrous mess of stinking flesh. The remains were so grotesque and mangled that deputies could only determine that it was a young black male. Closer examination produced the only clear mark of identification on the body: a silver ring with the inscription *May 25, 1943, L.T.* Mose Wright recognized it as the ring of Louis Till, Emmett's father, a ring that Emmett had worn.

After Mose Wright identified the body, Sheriff Strider gave orders to have it "in the ground before sundown," and Emmett's remains were sent to a black funeral home to be prepared for burial while workers began digging the grave.

The discovery of Emmett's body triggered a flurry of action. Sheriff Smith added murder to the charges against Bryant and Milam. *The Greenwood Commonwealth* prepared the headline "Missing Chicago Negro Youth Found in Tallahatchie River" for its afternoon edition. Curtis Jones called Chicago to notify Mrs. Bradley that Tallahatchie County authorities had found Emmett's body and planned to bury it as soon as possible.

Her family was with her when Mrs. Bradley received the tragic news, and everyone became hysterical. Though nearly overcome with grief, she knew she had to think clearly and take the right action. She told her relatives that there was no time for crying and immediately started working on getting Emmett's body shipped home. "It's something we've got to do," she told them. She contacted A. A. Rayner, their local mortician, and asked him to find a way to have Emmett's body returned to Chicago. Rayner and several other people began calling Mississippi officials to stop the burial and to have the body put on the next train headed north.

The grave was almost finished when Rayner finally received approval to block the quick burial. A Mississippi relative, Crosby Smith, gave the information to Sheriff Strider, who grudgingly acknowledged the orders to stop the burial and

Emmett's mother overcome with grief at a Chicago train station after seeing her son's coffin

to have the body prepared for interstate shipment. The sheriff agreed to send the body to Illinois on the condition that the casket remained sealed.

"Thank God for a divine being," said Mrs. Bradley years later. "I can truthfully say that from the day I knew Emmett was missing, that divine presence moved in . . . and it told me, 'I will lead you; I will guide you. Just obey.' Every time I got to a crisis, I got that message.

"We were able to get that body out of Mississippi, and I guess if we stopped and screamed ten minutes the body would have been buried while we were screaming. But that same little voice told me, 'You do not have time to cry now.

You will cry later. The world will cry for Emmett Till. Get the body out of Mississippi.' And that's what I did."

When the casket was delivered to the Chicago mortuary, Mrs. Bradley had it opened to make sure it really did contain her son. "When I looked at Emmett," she said, "I could not believe that it was even something human I was looking at. I was forced to do a bit-by-bit analysis on his entire body to make really sure that that was my son. If there was any way to disclaim that body, I would have sent that body back to Mississippi. But it was without a doubt Emmett.

"That was my darkest moment, when I realized that that huge box had the remains of my son."

A. A. Rayner had arranged for Emmett's Chicago funeral to take place on Saturday, September 3, but the day before the scheduled event, Mrs. Bradley decided to "Let the people see what they did to my boy," and requested an open-casket viewing. So many thousands of mourners thronged the viewing that the funeral had to be delayed until the following Tuesday. *The Chicago Defender* had already been covering the murder case, and it devoted even more intense print and photo coverage to the condition of Emmett Till's body and the effect it had on the crowds who saw it. *Jet,* an African American national weekly news magazine, launched the case to national prominence when it published an article about the murder case that included a close-up photo of Emmett's disfigured head. People across the nation then joined those in Chicago and Mississippi in their outrage over the brutal murder of the fourteen-year-old boy.

As a large crowd of family members and supporters watched, Emmett Till was finally laid to rest in Burr Oak Cemetery in Aslip, Illinois, on Tuesday, September 6. On the same day in Mississippi, a grand jury in Tallahatchie

County issued what many people considered an unprecedented decision: They indicted two white men for the murder of a black boy. The indictment read, in part, "Roy Bryant and J. W. Milam did willfully, unlawfully, feloniously, and of their malice aforethought did kill and murder Emmett Till, a human being, against the peace and dignity of the State of Mississippi." The grand jury's announcement stunned racist Mississippians and amazed Mississippi's black community.

Could justice be done in one of the most notoriously racist states in America? Both sides immediately began to gear up for the biggest trial in the history of the state of Mississippi.

The historic legal battle would start on Monday, September 19, 1955.

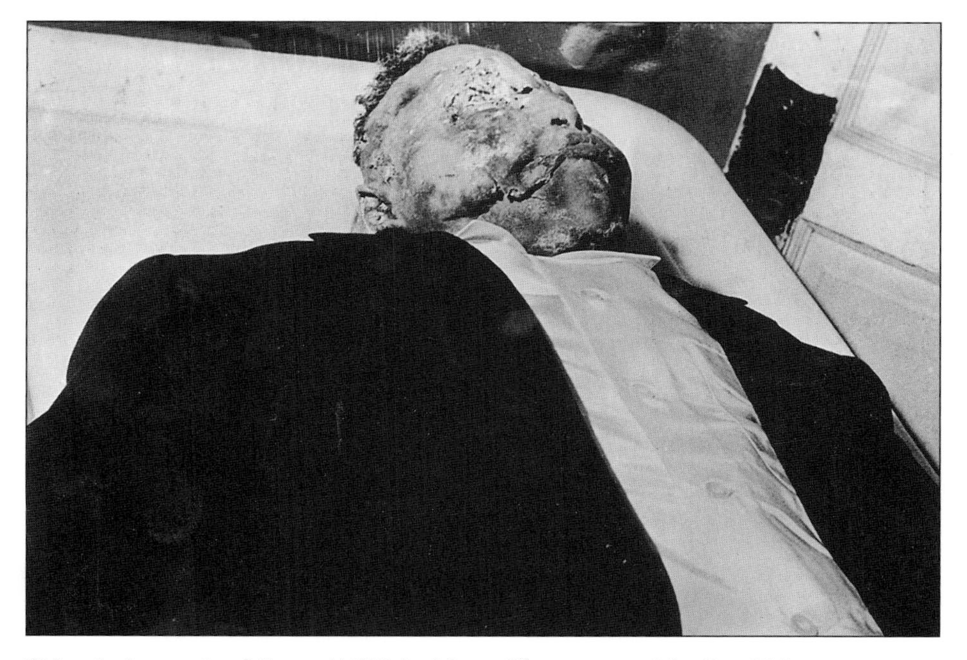

This photograph of Emmett Till in his coffin appeared in the African American Newspaper *The Chicago Defender*

THE GREENWOOD COMMONWEALTH
Missing Chicago Negro Youth Found in Tallahatchie River

August 31, 1955

The body of a 14-year-old kidnaped Chicago negro boy was found floating in the Tallahatchie River this morning. Discovery of the body was made by a young fisherman named [Hodges], who was inspecting his trot line. The body was in shallow water near the bank, it was reported, and was found at Pecan Point near Phillipp.

[Robert Hodges] notified Sheriff H. C. Strider at Charleston in Tallahatchie county of his find. He immediately called the sheriff's office in Greenwood and reported the matter.

Deputy Sheriff John Edd Cothran and Deputy Sheriff Ed Weber went to the scene and carried Mose Wright, uncle of the youth, along in order to make identification of the body. It was brought back to Greenwood and turned over to the Century Burial Association, local negro undertakers.

Officers said that the body had been weighted down with a cotton gin pulley tied with barbed wire. There was also a bullet hole in his head.

Three white men and a woman took the boy from his uncle's home early Sunday after the boy allegedly made "ugly remarks" to a white woman.

Two white men, Roy Bryant and his half brother J.W. Milam, have been charged with kidnaping. The sheriff's office said that an additional charge of murder will be made since the turn of events.

Sheriff George W. Smith said several days ago after the happening that he was afraid of foul play.

Young Till allegedly made the ugly remarks to Mrs. Bryant, wife of the storekeeper who faces a kidnaping charge. The youth was visiting his uncle, Mose Wright, a tenant farmer.

Sheriff Smith said Bryant admitted taking the boy from his uncle's home but said the youth was released when Mrs. Bryant said he was not the boy who made the remarks to her.

Sheriff Smith said the investigation showed:

Young Till and several other negro youths went to the Bryant store in the Money community and Till went in and allegedly made the remarks.

Early Sunday, a car carrying three men and a woman drove up to Wright's house. One of the men asked Wright if the boy from Chicago was there. Two men brought the boy out of the house.

Wright asked where they were taking his nephew. One of the men replied, "Nowhere if he's not the right one."

CHAPTER 5

SETTING THE STAGE

The announcement of the murder indictment and the trial date triggered widely publicized reactions from the North and the South.

Roy Wilkins, head of the NAACP, condemned the killing and the killers, calling the murder another example of white supremacist violence in the South. Civil rights supporters wrote to the governor of Mississippi demanding vigorous prosecution in the case, and the mayor of Chicago called on federal officials to join the investigation. Mrs. Mamie Till Bradley told reporters in Chicago that she was going to seek legal assistance to support the prosecution of the killers and that "Mississippi is going to pay for this." Southern newspapers reported only the latter part of her statement, making it look like Emmett's mother blamed the entire state of Mississippi for her son's murder. In a television interview just before the trial, Mrs. Bradley also demanded support from President Eisenhower: "It's my opinion that the guilt begins with Mrs. Bryant, and I want to see Mrs. Bryant, her husband, and any other persons that were in on this thing. And I feel like the pressure should start with the president of the United States and be channeled all the way down to the township of Money, Mississippi."

In Mississippi, Sheriffs Smith and Strider received letters and phone calls threatening them and Bryant and Milam; as a precaution, Smith called on National Guard troops to patrol the Leflore County jail. Strider reported rumors that thousands of African Americans were on their way to Mississippi to "tear up the jail and take the two men," but the threats didn't worry the Southern sheriff. He told *The Greenwood Commonwealth,* "These folks seem to think they are coming down here to take over—I don't think they are."

Robert Patterson, founder of the White Citizens' Council, said the Emmett Till murder couldn't be blamed on the Councils or any other segregationist group. "One of the primary reasons for our organization," he said, "is to prevent acts of violence. We are doing our best in spite of constant agitation and inflammatory statements from the NAACP and outside agitators." Defending his state against these outside agitators, Mississippi's governor, Hugh White, sent a telegram to the NAACP with this message: "Parties charged with the murder are in jail. I have every reason to believe that the court will do their duty in prosecution. Mississippi does not condone such conduct."

Before the widespread condemnation of Mississippi, local authorities looked forward to prosecuting the two brothers for Emmett's murder, and the sheriffs' offices in Leflore and Tallahatchie counties had been gathering evidence for the prosecution. Despite the state's violent racist culture, the vicious murder horrified many white residents, and they supported a conviction of Bryant and Milam. Neither of the killers was well liked in the community, and many people felt the brothers had overstepped their "white" authority in kidnapping and killing the boy. Initial public reaction in the Delta was so negative that no lawyer in the county would agree to defend the two men.

But the deluge of phone calls, letters, and telegrams from "outside agitators" and the loud criticism from Northern media put the local Mississippians, already on edge because of the *Brown v. Board of Education* decision, on the defensive. The hostile reaction against Mississippi convinced many white citizens that Southern culture was in danger, and they were determined to preserve their way of life at all costs. So, even though most white residents loathed siding with two unpopular "rednecks," on the weekend of September 3, 1955, public opinion in Leflore and Tallahatchie counties turned in favor of Bryant and Milam.

Sheriff Strider began a public defense of the killers when he announced to the press that he thought the body found in the Tallahatchie was much too old to be Emmett Till's and suggested that the boy was still alive. Strider later admitted privately, "The last thing I wanted to do was to defend those peckerwoods. But I just had no choice about it." That same weekend other county leaders also had a change of heart, and all five lawyers in the town of Sumner—J. J. Breland, C. Sidney Carlton, Harvey Henderson, J. W. Kellum, and John Whitten—agreed to take Bryant and Milam's case. Breland defended their decision by explaining that the lawyers felt the local murder case had turned into a media event pitting Mississippi and its way of life against outside agitators bent on destroying the South. He said they all felt intense pressure to "let the North know that we are not going to put up with Northern negroes 'stepping over the line.' "

An article in *The Greenwood Commonwealth* reported a similar response among the white residents of Leflore and Tallahatchie counties:

> "The attitude of Sumner citizens seemed to be that the indictments were expected, but citizens also resented charges and influence of

During a break in the trial, J. W. Milam and Roy Bryant talk with their mother. At right is Carolyn Bryant.

> outside organizations, especially the National Association for the Advancement of Colored People.
>
> "Vernon Brett, Sumner wholesale groceryman, said 'justice should be done, but we resent the outside interference from northern negroes who don't know the facts.'
>
> "C. Sidney Carlton, a defense attorney for Bryant and Milam, said, 'the people of this area all regret that this awful thing happened. We don't condone such actions, but the people here are not convinced that the boys (Bryant and Milam) killed the negro boy.' "

In the *Delta Democrat-Times,* editor Hodding Carter wrote that he believed that some groups outside Mississippi were using the Till case as an opportunity to make the state look bad. In an editorial published before the trial, he warned that the intense negative reactions from groups in the North might make it impossible for any white juror to issue a fair and honest decision.

> "[Northern agitators] could make the prospective Mississippi jurors so angry at these blanket indictments of our white society that it would seem a confirmation to convict any member of it, no matter how anti-social he or she might be. Then the purpose would have been accomplished and Mississippi could go down in further ignominy as a snakepit where justice cannot prevail for each race alike."

As a lifelong Southerner, Carter anticipated the reaction of the jury members to the pressures from the North and the South and lamented the inevitable fallout that would come if the murder trial weren't run honestly. "If the courts in Mississippi are unable to accomplish justice in this matter," he said, "we will deserve the criticism we get."

The defense lawyers weren't worried about Northern criticism; they simply wanted their clients declared innocent. A victory in this case, they assumed, would be more than enough to silence the rabble-rousers from the North. And victory was assured even before the trial began because Bryant and Milam's attorneys knew they could rely on the racist beliefs of their fellow white citizens to win an acquittal in the case. The defense team simply had to provide the jury members with an easy out, a legal reason to declare the killers innocent of the murder charges and still save face in their community.

Lead defense attorney J. J. Breland went public with the defense's strategy, and by doing so made available to all potential jurors a way for them to vote against a conviction of Bryant and Milam: "The way I see it," Breland told *The Greenwood Commonwealth,* "the state has got to prove three things: 1. That the boy was murdered. 2. That it happened in the second judicial district of Tallahatchie County. 3. That Bryant and Milam did it. It's all circumstantial, which is okay when you're returning an indictment but quite different when you've got to prove it beyond a reasonable doubt."

Then Breland did some public relations work to rebuild the image of the two "peckerwoods" he had agreed to defend. He said that he'd known his clients for several years, and that they were "men of good reputation, respected businessmen in the community, what I'd call real patriots, 100 percent Americans."

The pretrial publicity from Breland and Sheriff Strider and the increasingly hostile attacks from Northern and liberal media would send members of the jury into the trial with their minds made up. Like most Mississippi whites, they already believed they had to defend Southern society against "radicals" and "agitators" determined to force integration on their state. If jurors needed further reasons to acquit Bryant and Milam, they only had to recall Breland's preview of the defense's trial strategy, his certification of Bryant and Milam as "patriots," and Sheriff Strider's rumor that Emmett Till was still alive. That would give any white who served on the jury enough "evidence" to render a decision that would defend the South.

To its credit, the state did what it could to set up a fair trial by appointing one of Mississippi's leading prosecutors, District Attorney Gerald Chatham, to handle the trial, and by assigning Mississippi Assistant Attorney General Robert B. Smith, a former FBI agent, to assist Chatham in the case. The governor also assigned two additional attorneys and two Highway Patrol inspectors to help in the investigation. Circuit Judge Curtis M. Swango, widely respected for his fairness, presided at the trial that, by his order, would begin on Monday, September 19.

The site of the famous trial was the Tallahatchie County courthouse, a sturdy pre–World War I stone building that occupied the center of the town square of Sumner, Mississippi, population 550. On the morning of September 19, throngs of people, black and white, Northerner and Southerner, jammed the square, waiting for the trial to begin. More than seventy photographers and newspaper, radio, and television reporters from all over the United States were among the crowd.

Sheriff Strider reminded Northern reporters that the courtroom was segregated, just like every other public building in the state. "We've kept the races separated for a long time," he said, "and we don't intend to change now." When the county building opened its doors for the trial, more than 250 whites were allowed to file upstairs to the second-floor courtroom. After the whites had their

Scene of the trial: the Tallahatchie County courthouse in Sumner, Mississippi

seats, deputies let about fifty African American spectators enter and sit in the back of the court, and despite the protests of Sheriff Strider, Judge Swango permitted eight African American reporters to be seated at a card table set up in the rear of the courtroom. In the front of the courtroom facing the judge's stand, Bryant and Milam sat at a table with their lawyers. The defendants' wives and mother sat behind them. Each defendant had two young sons, and the four little boys split time between their mothers' laps and their fathers'.

By the time the trial began, about 350 spectators were crammed into the courtroom designed for only 280 people, and an overflow crowd of nearly 1,000 waited outside on the courthouse lawn to receive regular updates on the trial.

Despite the seriousness of the event and the heat and humidity of a late summer Delta heat wave, the courtroom buzzed with excitement. Ruby Hurley, an NAACP worker who attended the trial, recalled the scene: "It was just like a circus. The defendants were sitting up there eating ice-cream cones and playing with their children in court just like they were out at a picnic. Everybody was searched going into the courtroom to make sure none of the Negroes carried weapons." Even though deputies had searched most people who attended the trial, many of the black spectators worried about becoming targets of violence

J. W. Milam and Roy Bryant in court with their sons

from resentful whites. Some of the black journalists had even worked out an escape plan they could use if gunfire broke out.

The courtroom atmosphere and the unfair treatment of African Americans in the audience foreshadowed a number of departures from standard legal practice that would occur during the weeklong trial in Sumner, Mississippi. The procedural inconsistencies, however, would have no effect on the trial's outcome; according to nearly everyone involved in the case, even before the trial began, no one in Sumner doubted that Bryant and Milam would be declared not guilty.

Judge Swango called the court to order and directed the lawyers on both sides to begin interviewing prospective jurors. Hoping to prevent jury candidates from excusing themselves because of a reluctance to use capital punishment, prosecuting attorney Chatham startled everyone in the room when he announced that the state would not seek the death penalty. "A substantial part of the state's evidence is circumstantial evidence," he said. "This case has received wide publicity. The state is going to take every precaution to see that we have a fair and impartial jury." His surprising announcement drew such a stir from the audience that Judge Swango had to bang his gavel repeatedly to restore order.

Even in jury selection, Chatham faced an uphill battle. Mississippi state law required that only registered male voters who were at least twenty-one years old and could read and write were eligible for jury duty. Even though 63 percent of the residents of Tallahatchie County were black, the pool of prospective jurors contained only white men because Tallahatchie County had no black registered voters. Chatham knew in advance that the jury would be all white, but he hoped that he could convince the jurors that race wasn't an issue in the trial. As far as he was concerned, murder was murder; the race of the killers and the victim was irrelevant. In addressing all the prospective jurors, he stressed that the state wanted a fair and impartial jury and asked them to put aside "any prejudice because the defendants are members of the white race and the deceased was a member of the colored race."

Interviewing and selecting jurors took all day, and the audience watched restlessly while lawyers carefully questioned jury candidates. Even with the case stacked in their favor, the defense attorneys relied on input from Sheriff Strider, who knew almost everyone in the county, to select men who would be friendly to their cause. Strider's recommendations and J. J. Breland's questions helped his team select jurors who would play along with the defense's approach to the trial. Breland identified jurors who would be sympathetic to Bryant and Milam by asking "Will you be sure beyond a *reasonable doubt* that the dead body found in the river was Emmett Till?"

The prosecution's questions took a different approach. Chatham and Smith asked candidates if they were racially prejudiced, if they were personal friends of Bryant or Milam, or if they had contributed to the defense fund. Many candidates were disqualified by their answers or by challenges from the defense, but after interviewing more than fifty men, both sides finally agreed on twelve men

From left to right: Tallahatchie County Attorney J. Hamilton Caldwell, District Attorney Gerald Chatham, and Special Prosecutor Robert Smith III

Sheriff H. C. Strider, standing at right, addresses the jury that would determine the fate of J. W. Milam and Roy Bryant

and one alternate for the jury. Court adjourned at 4:30 Monday afternoon, and spectators filed out of the stuffy, crowded courtroom anxious to return for the next day's action.

Tuesday's trial highlight was the entrance of Emmett's mother, accompanied by Charles C. Diggs Jr., one of the few African Americans in the United States Congress at the time. The crowd turned quiet as Mamie Till Bradley entered the courtroom and was seated at the black press table in the rear. Deputies blocked Representative Diggs from entering, and when he identified himself as a member of Congress who had received permission from Judge Swango to attend the trial, one deputy couldn't believe what he had heard. "Hell, that ain't even legal," he exclaimed. Eventually Diggs was searched and allowed to enter.

Not long after Mrs. Bradley was seated, Sheriff Strider pushed his way through the crowd and handed her a subpoena to testify in the trial. She accepted it without speaking.

The courtroom audience, which had swelled to almost four hundred people on Tuesday morning, was disappointed when Chatham asked the judge for a recess to allow him and his assistants to search for and question potential witnesses that Medgar Evers and other NAACP workers had been trying to locate. Chatham's request and the overcrowded courtroom conditions prompted Judge Swango to recess court until Wednesday morning. Bryant and Milam's lawyers, confident of victory no matter what evidence or testimony the prosecution presented, were frustrated by what they considered Chatham's stalling tactics.

Chatham, like everyone else in Mississippi, knew the defense's plan relied on creating reasonable doubt about the identity of the killers and the body. He hoped that eyewitness testimony might be so irrefutable that even a white, racist jury would have to vote to convict Bryant and Milam of murder. Various sources in the Delta had reported to Chatham that at least two African American men, Leroy "Too Tight" Collins and Henry Lee Loggins, might have been witnesses to the murder and that other people would be able to testify that they had seen these men with Emmett Till after the kidnapping or with Bryant and Milam on the morning of the murder. A newspaper article reported on the potential witnesses, but unfortunately for the prosecution, these men were never found. (Unbeknownst to Chatham's team, shortly after the murder indictment against Bryant and Milam, Sheriff Strider had had Collins and Loggins locked up in the Charleston jail under false identities; they remained there until after the trial.)

Chatham's assistants were finally able to locate three new witnesses who agreed to appear in court. Several other African American farm workers who had been interviewed by Medgar Evers and his assistants might have provided important testimony against Bryant and Milam, but they refused to show up at the trial because they feared for their lives. All of them knew that testifying against a white man would ruin—or end—their lives in the Delta.

Finally, the investigative work of Chatham's team was finished. The actors were all in place, and the stage was set for the evidence and testimony portion of the tense and widely publicized courtroom drama.

CHAPTER 6

GETTING AWAY WITH MURDER

Judge Swango opened court Wednesday morning by reminding the audience about proper courtroom etiquette and by scolding several photographers for taking pictures while court was in session. That would not be his last warning to spectators, reporters, and photographers to abide by proper courtroom etiquette, and it's ironic that while the judge vigorously policed audience behavior throughout the trial, he allowed some judicial proceedings to occur that were both illogical and inconsistent with standard legal practice. Despite those inconsistencies, however, Judge Swango would conduct the trial in a way that earned him the respect of almost everyone involved in the case.

After the judge finished admonishing the audience, the trial finally began. Before calling his first witness, Chatham faced the jury and announced, "The state has found six new witnesses who will place the defendants with the Negro boy several hours after he was taken from Mose Wright's home. These witnesses will present absolutely newly discovered evidence that will convince you,

An overhead view of the courtroom during a recess in the trial. African American spectators, required to sit at the back of the room, do not appear in this photograph.

beyond a shadow of a doubt, that Roy Bryant and J. W. Milam kidnapped and murdered the child named Emmett Till."

The state's first witness, Mose Wright, had to push his way through the crowded courtroom to get to the witness stand. The chair was almost too big for the small man, and under the hateful glares of hundreds of hostile spectators, he sat uncomfortably on its edge, waiting for his opportunity to testify. Chatham began by asking Wright to describe what had happened on August 28.

Wright straightened up in the chair and told how two men had come to his front door that Sunday around 2:00 A.M. One of them said, "This is Mr. Bryant," and then demanded to see "the boy who done that talk at Money." Wright said that when he opened the door, Milam stood there with a pistol and a flashlight; another man stood beside Milam in the shadows.

Wright continued his story, but Chatham interrupted him to ask, "Uncle Mose, do you see Mr. Milam in the courtroom?"

The audience fell silent, wondering if Wright would risk his life to accuse a white man in open court. For a moment no one moved. Excruciating tension filled the room while people waited for Wright's reply. Then, in one of the most dramatic moments in Mississippi trial history, Mose Wright, a poor black sharecropper, stood up, raised his arm, pointed at Milam, a white man, and said, "There he is." Wright then pointed at Bryant, identifying him as the man who had assisted Milam in the kidnapping. Wright later said that while he was on the witness stand, he could "feel the blood boil in hundreds of white people as they sat glaring in the courtroom. It was the first time in my life I had the courage to accuse a white man of a crime, let alone something terrible as killing a boy. I wasn't exactly brave and I wasn't scared. I just wanted to see justice done."

Murray Kempton, a reporter for the *New York Post*, admired Wright's courage. Kempton wrote that after Wright singled out Milam and Bryant, he "sat down hard against the chairback with a lurch which told better than anything else the cost in strength to him of the thing he had done. He was a field Negro who had dared try to send two white men to the gas chamber for murdering a Negro. [He] had come to the end of the hardest half hour in the hardest life possible for a human being in these United States."

After identifying the two killers, Wright, who, at that moment, exiled himself from Mississippi forever, responded to the rest of Chatham's questions with a firm, confident voice, detailing the fateful events that began the night Bryant and Milam pushed their way into his house and ended the day Wright

During his testimony, Mose Wright stands and points out the two men who kidnapped Emmett Till

identified Emmett Till's body on the banks of the Tallahatchie River. Wright was able to identify the body, he said, from Emmett's father's ring, which the boy was wearing.

When Chatham finished his questions, defense attorney Sidney Carlton quickly started his cross-examination. He challenged Wright's ability to recognize the two men in the darkness. Carlton hammered away at Wright's testimony, but Wright refused to change his answers, insisting that he was confident that he had correctly identified Bryant and Milam as the kidnappers of Emmett Till.

After Wright was excused from the witness stand, Chatham called on Sheriff George Smith to testify that Roy Bryant had confessed to kidnapping Emmett. Smith reported that Bryant "told me he went down there to Wright's shack and brought Till up to Bryant's store and he wasn't the right one and he turned him loose." The defense had no questions for Sheriff Smith.

Key evidence: Emmett's father's ring, which Emmett was wearing at the time of his death

The next witness was Chester Miller, an undertaker from the Century Burial Association, a black mortuary in Greenwood. Local authorities had called Miller to be present when they retrieved Emmett's body from the river. Under Chatham's questioning, Miller described the condition of the body: "The whole top of the head was crushed in. A piece of the skull fell out in the boat. I saw a hole in his skull about one inch above the right ear." Defense attorneys Breland and Carlton constantly shouted objections during Miller's testimony, and he sometimes became distracted or confused by the loud objections and the stream of questions from Chatham. Miller's discomfort caused the disrespectful white audience to break into laughter several times, and each time, Judge Swango pounded his gavel and demanded quiet from the spectators. When Miller was finished, a white undertaker, C. F. Nelson, also testified about the condition of the body.

C. A. Strickland from the Greenwood Police Department was Wednesday's last witness. He told the court about police photographs of Emmett's corpse and of the scene where Emmett's body had been recovered. The defense objected to the admission of some of the photographs as evidence because the captions contained inaccuracies. Their objections were sustained, and the sensational day of testimony adjourned at 2:30 to give lawyers on both sides an opportunity to interview the new witnesses discovered by Chatham's investigators.

The most poignant moments of the trial came during Mamie Till Bradley's testimony Thursday morning. A hush fell over the courtroom when Chatham called her to the stand and she walked resolutely to the front of the courtroom from her seat at the black press table in the back. The circumstances must have been nearly unbearable for her. Her son had disappeared about a month earlier. Then his mutilated body was discovered, identified, and shipped home. She had collapsed at the train station when she opened the casket. A three-day viewing was followed by a huge funeral. Through all of these ordeals, Mrs. Bradley had to mourn the violent and senseless death of her only child, while at the same time helping to mount an effort to see his killers punished. Despite the inestimable stresses she felt at the trial, she remained remarkably poised and clear-headed. A white local newspaper reporter described her as a "fashionably dressed 33-year-old negro woman" who displayed "an air of confidence and determination. Her answers were direct and to the point, using good English and speaking in a highly audible tone."

Many whites in the courtroom were surprised to see a composed, articulate black woman in such a hostile environment, and it was clear to everyone that Emmett's mother would not be intimidated. Even though most white spectators resented her presence at the trial, the defense team made a show of treating her civilly when she was first introduced as a witness. It was so unusual in the South for white men to treat an African American woman with respect that their actions caught the attention of a newspaper reporter who wrote: "She was shown every courtesy by both counsel for the prosecution and defense. At no time was she shouted at during testimony."

Emmett's mother took her seat facing the two men who had murdered her son, two men surrounded by their family and supporters. The killers ignored her as Chatham started his questions.

"Mrs. Bradley," he asked, "when your son's body arrived in Chicago, were you able to identify it as him?"

"Yes, sir, positively," she replied without hesitation. She explained that because of the horrible condition of her son's body, she began her examination with his feet. Then she studied his hands, his teeth and gums, and his hairline. "A mother knows her child," she said, "has known him since he was born. I looked at the face very carefully . . . I just looked at it very carefully, and I was able to find out that it was my son, Emmett Louis Till."

Chatham then showed her a photograph of the body taken at the Century

Burial Association after Emmett had been removed from the Tallahatchie River on August 31. He asked her if she could identify the body in the photo.

She looked at it and nodded. "That's my son, my son, Emmett Till." Her voice broke, and she took off her glasses to wipe away tears.

"Are you sure?" Chatham asked.

"If I thought it wasn't my boy, I would be out looking for him now."

When Chatham finished questioning Emmett's mother, the defense lawyers had their turn. From his seat at the defense table, Breland fired questions at Mrs. Bradley, disputing her ability to identify the body found in the river as her son. A lawyer showed her a photo from *The Chicago Defender* of Emmett in his coffin and challenged her to explain how she could recognize the disfigured corpse. Mrs. Bradley held steadfast to her testimony despite defense attorneys' efforts to make her admit uncertainty about the identity of the remains. "Beyond a shadow of a doubt," she affirmed, "that was my son's body."

Many years later, Mamie Till Bradley recalled that day in court. "I remember I was concentrating very hard on using the proper language, the 'yes, sirs' and the 'no, sirs,'" she said. "And I was certainly not treated very gentle on this day and on the witness stand. Particularly when I was so adamant about that being Emmett's body. I knew that if they could just get me to say this wasn't Emmett, they could get off scot-free. But I couldn't say that, because I knew that was Emmett."

Eighteen-year-old Willie Reed took the witness stand next. The son of a black sharecropper had the courage of the previous black witnesses but lacked the composure of Mose Wright and Mamie Till Bradley. Facing a large audience of antagonistic white people intimidated him, and several times during Reed's testimony Judge Swango had to admonish the teenager to speak more loudly.

Under Prosecutor Smith's questioning, Reed said that at around 8:00 A.M., Sunday, August 28, he saw four white men and two black men drive up to a barn on the plantation owned by Leslie Milam, J. W. Milam's brother, in nearby Sunflower County. The two black men rode in the back of the pickup with Emmett Till. When the truck stopped, the men carried Emmett into the barn, from where Willie later heard screams and "licks and hollering."

Over the defense's repeated objections, Reed testified that when he heard the screams, he ran to the home of his aunt, Amanda Bradley, who lived on the plantation, and asked, "Who are they beating to death down at the barn, Aunt Mandy?" Not long after that, Reed saw J. W. Milam, with a pistol on his hip, leave the barn to get water from the well. A few moments later Milam was joined by three other white men.

Reed said that after he heard the screams and saw Milam and the other men, he went to a country store and then returned home to get ready for Sunday school.

"On the way back, did you hear anything or anybody?" Smith asked.

"No, sir," answered Reed.

"Was the truck gone?"

"Yes, sir."

Reed's testimony presented a threat to the defense's "reasonable doubt" strategy, and Bryant and Milam's lawyers moved quickly to undermine Reed's statements. First they tried to create doubt that Reed even knew who J. W. Milam was. Reed stated that he had seen Milam three or four times but had never before seen that pickup truck.

"Was Mr. J. W. Milam driving the truck?" a defense lawyer asked.

"No, sir," said Reed.

"Did you see Mr. Milam in the truck?"

In preparation for his testimony, Willie Reed, center, talks with Gerald Chatham

"No, sir."

"You wouldn't say Mr. Milam was inside the truck?"

"No, sir, I wouldn't," Reed answered.

Then, in an effort to weaken the credibility of Reed's testimony, the defense asked a series of questions about how far Reed had been from the truck when he first saw it, and how far he was from the barn when he saw Milam leave the barn to get a drink. The threatening pressure from the defense lawyer caused Reed to stumble in his testimony, and he admitted that he didn't know exactly how far away he had been from the men. Seeing a chance to cast a cloud of doubt over Reed's testimony, the defense continued to press the boy about the distances involved. After a barrage of questions that rattled the teenager's confidence, Reed finally guessed that he had observed the men from a distance of about four hundred yards.

When the defense finished its cross-examination, Prosecutor Smith asked Reed a final question. "Did you see [Milam] before you heard the noise in the barn and the hollering?"

"After I heard it," replied Reed.

With Willie Reed's testimony over, Judge Swango recessed court until

Willie Reed testified that he heard "licks and hollering" coming from this building on Leslie Milam's plantation

1:30 P.M. Reed quickly left the court building and was rushed out of town by Congressman Diggs. For his own safety, Reed would flee Mississippi soon after the trial.

After the lunch recess, four witnesses testified for the prosecution. Fifty-year-old Mary Amanda Bradley, Willie Reed's aunt, told the jury that she saw four white men going in and out of Leslie Milam's barn, where Reed said he had heard the screams and beating. Reed's grandfather Add Reed reported that he had seen Leslie Milam at the plantation that same morning.

The final two witnesses for the state took the stand over objections from Bryant and Milam's lawyers. Leflore County Sheriff George Smith told the court that Roy Bryant had admitted to him that he had kidnapped Emmett from his uncle's home but that he had released him unharmed later that night. Deputy Sheriff John Edd Cothran testified that J. W. Milam had also confessed to having abducted Emmett. The lawmen's testimony combined with Mose Wright's made obvious what everyone in the courtroom already knew: Roy Bryant and his half brother, J. W. Milam, had kidnapped Emmett Till early in the morning of August 28. Unfortunately for the prosecution, the two men were on trial for murder, and none of the witnesses had testified that they had actually seen Bryant and Milam kill the boy; it would take that kind of direct testimony from a white Southern man to convince this jury to convict the two brothers.

At 1:56 P.M., emotionally and physically exhausted, and without any more witnesses or evidence to support the state's case against Bryant and Milam, Gerald Chatham told Judge Swango that the prosecution had finished its presentation.

As soon as Chatham sat down, the defense attorneys asked Judge Swango to end the case immediately by declaring Bryant and Milam not guilty. The judge rejected their request, and it then became the defense's turn to make their case.

Defense attorney Sidney Carlton called Carolyn Bryant, wife of Roy Bryant and the woman who had been "molested" by the boy from Chicago, as their first witness.

Before Judge Swango allowed Carlton to question Mrs. Bryant, he dismissed the jury because, he explained, too much time had elapsed between the incident at the store in Money and the kidnapping. Her testimony was, however, included in the official court record.

This was the kind of show many of the whites in the audience had come for. They leaned forward in their seats to better hear all the juicy details of the alleged assault that had taken place at Bryant's store. As the spectators listened, Mrs. Bryant told how a black man with a Northern accent had molested her in the store a few days before Emmett Till was kidnapped.

"This negro man came into the store," she said, "and stopped at the candy counter." He asked for bubble gum, she told the jury. "I held out my right hand for some money and he caught my hand. I pulled away and he said, 'How about a date, baby?'"

The courtroom audience turned dead silent, the air hot with hatred.

"I turned and started to the back of the store," she continued, "but he caught me at the cash register . . . and put both hands around my waist. He said, 'What's the matter, baby, can't you take it? You needn't be afraid of me.'" While the sympathetic white audience listened, horrified and furious, Mrs. Bryant said she wrenched herself out of his grasp, and when she did, the man said unprintable words to her, filthy words she refused to repeat in court. The last thing he told her was, "I've been with white women before."

At that point, she said, another black man came in and pulled the first man out of the store. "I started out for my pistol," she said, "and he was standing on the front porch of the store. He whistled."

Mrs. Bryant's testimony would have been enough for nearly any white jury in Mississippi at the time to justify the murder. Southern womanhood had been assaulted, they would have rationalized, and the woman's husband had no choice but to kill the perpetrator. White racists believed it was the only way to protect white women and to keep "those people" in their places. The jury didn't need to hear her testimony, however, because they, like everyone else in the county, already knew what had happened. The story of the alleged assault in Bryant's store had been all the evidence most white citizens in the area needed to decide that Emmett Till got what he deserved.

The jury reentered after Carolyn Bryant's testimony and heard briefly from Juanita Milam, J. W. Milam's wife. Then the defense called its surprise witness, Sheriff H. C. Strider.

Sheriff Strider followed the defense strategy exactly. His goal was to convince the jury that it would have been impossible for anyone to positively identify the body, thus giving the jury enough reasonable doubt that Emmett Till was really dead to acquit Bryant and Milam. Strider testified that based on his previous experience, the body found in the Tallahatchie River on August 31 had been in the river for at least ten to twenty days. He said that the corpse was so decomposed that it was impossible for him to recognize the victim or even determine if the body was black or white. "If one of my own boys was missing, I couldn't really say if it was my own son or not, or anybody else's. . . . All I could tell, it was a human being."

The prosecution let Strider's testimony go unchallenged, but during a break in the proceedings, Clotye Murdock Larsson, an African American reporter covering the trial, angrily approached the judge to contest what Strider had said. "I pushed my way through the milling crowd of Whites," she recalled, "and asked Judge Curtis Swango . . . why, if Sheriff Strider was unsure of the victim's racial identity, he had asked a Black undertaker to take charge of the body!" Larsson received no reply, only angry stares from whites that made it clear she had risked her life to make that sort of accusation in their presence.

Two local experts, a white doctor who reported that he had viewed the body at a distance because of the smell, and a white embalmer who had helped prepare the body for shipment to Chicago, both backed up Strider's statement. The two men said that the body they had examined was so decomposed that it must have been dead for at least ten days before it had been found. It was, said the embalmer, "bloated beyond recognition." Their statements concluded Thursday's activities, and Judge Swango rapped his gavel on his desk, closing court for the day.

Nature provided an appropriate setting for the final day of the trial. Early Friday morning, a huge thunderstorm rocked Tallahatchie County. The storm ended before the last day's events began, making the air in the crowded and cramped courtroom hotter and heavier than ever before.

With Chatham and Smith watching, the defense began their presentation by interviewing five character witnesses who testified to Milam's impressive record in World War II, of Bryant's military service, and of the two men's good reputations. After the last witness, Breland told Judge Swango that the defense rested. Soon, both sides would deliver their final arguments.

After a brief recess, Chatham began his closing argument, a rousing oration that would last for almost an hour. Sweating profusely and with his sleeves rolled up, he raised his arm over his head and shouted to the jury, "They murdered that boy, and to hide that dastardly, cowardly act, they tied barbed wire to his neck and to a heavy gin fan and dumped him in the river for the turtles and the fish." Chatham then reviewed all the evidence and testimony presented in the case, including the eyewitness testimony that showed beyond a

A deputy shows the gin fan used to sink Emmett's body in the river

doubt that Bryant and Milam had kidnapped Emmett Till. He also reminded the jury that this case was not about race or equality. It was about the murder of a boy.

Throughout Chatham's argument, Bryant and Milam showed little emotion. Reporter Dan Wakefield wrote that while Chatham spoke, "J. W. Milam, the bald, strapping man who leaned forward in his seat during most of the sessions with his mouth twisted in the start of a smile, was looking at a newspaper. Roy Bryant lit a cigar. With his eyebrows raised and his head tilted back he might have been a star college fullback smoking in front of his coach during the season and asking with his eyes, 'So what?'"

Ignoring the two defendants, Chatham continued his closing statement. "The first words that entered this case were literally dripping with the blood of Emmett Till," Chatham said in a booming voice. Then he rehashed the events of that August night when Emmett had been kidnapped. "As far as the state of Mississippi is concerned, this is not about race, it's just another murder. But I want to say to you that the murder of Emmett Till was a cowardly act and a brutal and unnecessary killing of a human being. His abduction at gunpoint was unjustified. This was a summary court martial with the death penalty. That child had done nothing that would cause the defendants to invade the privacy of that home.

"When those two defendants took Emmett Till from the home of Uncle Mose Wright, they were absolutely and morally responsible for his protection. I was born in the South. I'll live and die in the South. The very worst punishment that should have occurred, if they had any idea in their minds this boy did anything, would have been to take a razor strap, turn him over a barrel and give him a little beating. I've whipped my boy. You've whipped yours. A man deals with a child accordingly as a child, not as a man to a man." As Chatham spoke, the jury looked attentive but unmoved. The defense attorneys could not look Chatham in the face while he concluded his valiant effort to bring justice to the segregated courtroom in the Mississippi Delta by pleading with the jury to convict Bryant and Milam of murder. One of Chatham's last statements was a quotation from the twenty-eighth chapter of Proverbs that explained, in part, his reasons for prosecuting these two men: "The wicked flee when no man pursueth: but the righteous are bold as a lion."

Robert Smith made the final arguments for the prosecution. Hoping to convince the jurors that an acquittal in this case would further damage the state's reputation, he built his concluding argument on the defensiveness white Mississippians felt at the time. Facing the jury, he said, "I tell you, gentlemen, that Emmett Till was entitled to his constitutional rights; he was entitled to his liberty, and once we go taking away his rights, then we are on the defensive and we can't complain what people do to us. Those people, outside agitators, want J. W. Milam and Roy Bryant turned loose. If they're convicted, those people are silenced. They can't say the state of Mississippi didn't do its duty." His closing

J. W. Milam and Roy Bryant confer with one of their defense attorneys, Sidney Carlton

remarks finished, Smith joined Chatham at the prosecution's table to wait out the remainder of the trial.

When it was their turn for closing arguments, the defense lawyers consistently worked to stir up Southern patriotism and racism in the jurors so they'd feel compelled to declare Bryant and Milam innocent. Attorney John Whitten told the jury, "There are people in the United States who want to destroy the custom and way of life of Southern white people and Southern colored people. There are people out to put us at odds, who are willing to go as far as possible, to commit any crime to widen the gap between us. They would not be above putting a rotting, stinking body in the river in the hope it would be identified as Emmett Till. If these people had the opportunity to create a commotion, to stir up a trial such as this and focus national attention on Mississippi and focus national attention on the strained relations here, they would do it." Whitten concluded by reminding them that "every last Anglo-Saxon one of you men in this jury has the courage to set these men free."

Sidney Carlton, who throughout the trial had played to the media as much as to the jury, went next. He emphasized again and again that the state had failed to prove the identity of the body beyond a reasonable doubt. The prosecution had, he said, "talked generalities because the facts just didn't bear out the guilt of these defendants. Where's the motive?" he shouted. "Where's the motive?" Carlton contended that Mrs. Bryant's testimony about the black man who had assaulted her did not implicate Emmett Till, so there would have been no reason for Bryant and Milam to harm the boy. It was obvious, according to Carlton, that Emmett had *not* been the person in the store. "The state did not link up the dead boy with the defendants. The only testimony that Emmett Till did anything in connection with these defendants was Mose Wright's testimony that he heard the boy had done something. If [Mose Wright] *had* known Emmett Till had done something down there, he would have gotten him out and whipped him himself."

Carlton went on to question Mose Wright's ability to recognize the intruders who came into his home in the dark of the night. With only the light from the kidnappers' flashlight illuminating the unlit rooms, it would have been impossible, he claimed, for the old man to see either intruder's face clearly enough to recognize him. According to Carlton, Wright's account of what had been said by the two men was also impossible to believe. "Had any of you gone to Mose Wright's house with evil intent, would you have given your name? How many Mr. Bryants are there in the state of Mississippi? There's nothing reasonable about the state's theory. If that's identification, if that places these men at that scene," he shouted, "then none of us are safe!"

The concluding defense statements were delivered by J. W. Kellum, who told the jury, "I'll be waiting for you when you come out. If your verdict is guilty, I want you to come to me and tell me where is the land of the free and the home of the brave. I say to you, gentlemen, your forefathers will absolutely turn over in their graves if these boys were convicted on such evidence as this." He finished by saying that a guilty verdict would be admitting that freedom was lost forever, and then admonished the jury to "Turn these boys loose." Kellum's directive were the last words the jury heard from the defense.

At 2:34 P.M. Judge Swango sent the jury to the deliberation room to consider their verdict. While in the room, the jury cast three ballots, each one with the same result: unanimously not guilty. Their decision hadn't taken long, but they had been advised to take their time before coming back into the courtroom in order to make it look like they had actually deliberated their decision. They sent out for some Cokes, drank them at their leisure, and then returned to the courtroom just one hour and eight minutes after they had left.

Once they were seated, the jury foreman handed their verdict to the court clerk, Charlie Cox, who read it aloud for everyone to hear. "We, the jury, find the defendants not guilty."

The announcement triggered a loud celebration in the courtroom. Bryant and Milam shook hands and slapped backs with their lawyers; then they turned and kissed their wives. Somebody handed both men cigars, and photographers started snapping photos to capture the scene. Justice, racist style, had been done.

In the foyer after the trial, a TV reporter asked Sheriff Strider if it was true that he had received threats and hate mail ever since Bryant and Milam had been arrested.

"I'm glad you asked me this," replied the sheriff. "I just want to tell all those people who've been sending me threatening letters that if they ever come down here, the same thing's gonna happen to them that happened to Emmett Till."

Justice. Racist style.

> THE GREENWOOD COMMONWEALTH
> New Story On Murder Of Till
>
> MEMPHIS, Sept. 21 (AP)—The Memphis Press Scimitar said today it had been told that two negro men, last seen in the company of slain Emmett Till, had disappeared.
>
> The newspaper said reporter Clark Porteous also had unearthed information that could place the Till murder site in Sunflower County, Miss., instead of in Tallahatchie County where the trial of two white men accused of killing the young Chicago negro is under way.

After the verdict, J. W. Milam and Roy Bryant celebrate the jury's decision with their wives

Porteous, in a story written from Sumner, Miss., trial scene, said his new information had been obtained from Dr. T. R. M. Howard, a negro physician and a resident of the all-negro town of Mound Bayou, Miss.

Porteous quoted Howard as saying he could produce four or five witnesses "at the proper time" who would testify that Till's slaying "probably" occurred in the headquarters shed of a plantation near Drew, Miss. Drew is in Sunflower County.

Howard also said, Porteous wrote, that his informants told him they had seen four white men and three negroes, including Till, enter the shed in a truck in the early morning hours of Aug. 28. That was the day young Till was taken from the home of his uncle, Mose Wright, near Money, Miss.

Only the white men were seen in the truck when it left the shed, Howard said. A tarpaulin was spread over its pickup compartment, he said.

"There are witnesses," Howard said, "who heard the cries of a boy from the closed shed. They heard blows. They noted with anxiety of soul that the cries gradually decreased until they were heard no more."

Howard identified the two negroes reported missing as Leroy Collins and Henry Lee Loggins, plantation workers.

CHAPTER 7

AFTERSHOCKS

Southern racism won a battle in the Emmett Till case, but that would be one of its last victories in its war against integration and racial equality. The murder of a fourteen-year-old boy from Chicago and the trial of his killers would turn out to be the beginning of the decline of segregation and Jim Crow rule in the South.

While some reporters and well-wishers crowded around local "heroes" Roy Bryant and J. W. Milam in the noisy Sumner courtroom on Friday, September 23, other journalists were busily writing articles and headlines condemning the outcome of the trial. The bad news spread lightning-fast across the country. In a banner headline, one African American newspaper declared the day "Black Friday!" An NAACP news release to the Associated Press called the verdict "as shameful as it is shocking." Many African Americans and sympathetic whites were disgusted by the news of the acquittal and concerned that the victory signaled a continuation of racial discrimination in the South.

But not everyone felt so hopeless. An article in the *New York Post* denounced the biased decision of the Sumner jury but also predicted that the intense media coverage of the trial would have a positive effect on American life. "There can be no rest for Till's murderers," the paper stated, "or for those who have rationalized this brutal deed. Like other great episodes in the battle for equality and justice in America, this trial has rocked the world, and nothing can ever be quite the same again—even in Mississippi." Many people in the North and in the South hoped the newspaper's prediction would be right.

Immediately after the trial, civil rights activists used the momentum from the case to cultivate support. On Sunday, September 25, Charles C. Diggs Jr. and Medgar Evers spoke to a crowd of more than 60,000 people at a rally in Detroit; Roy Wilkins and Mamie Till Bradley addressed 15,000 in New York City; and Simeon Booker, an editor for *Jet* magazine, talked about the Emmett Till case to a gathering of over 10,000 people in Chicago. These protest rallies continued for several more weeks, earning financial and emotional backing for the NAACP and its fight against racism. Hundreds of thousands of people across the nation turned out for these meetings; by the end of 1955, Emmett's mother and Mose Wright themselves had spoken to more than 250,000 people.

In the meantime, the national press took up the cause. An editorial in *The Commonweal* reported on the murder and the trial, concluding that "By his death Emmett [sic] Louis Till took racism out of the textbooks and editorials and showed it to the world in its true dimensions. Now the ugliness is there for all the world to see." Other periodicals reacted to that ugliness. *Life* magazine published an editorial eulogizing Emmett with passionate, religious language. "Sleep well, Emmett Till," it read. "You will be avenged. You will be remembered as long as men have tongues to cry against evil." *Newsweek, Time,*

The Nation, The New Republic, and other national magazines published similar reactions to the murder and trial.

Even Nobel Prize–winning novelist William Faulkner condemned the racist killing. While on tour outside of the United States, he followed news reports of the case and told reporters, "Perhaps the purpose of this sorry and tragic error committed in my native Mississippi by two white adults on an afflicted Northern child is to prove to us whether or not we deserve to survive. Because if we in America have reached that point in our desperate culture when we must murder children, no matter for what reason or what color, we don't deserve to

Medgar Evers, State Secretary for the NAACP in Jackson, Mississippi, a few weeks before Emmett Till's murder

Emmett's mother surrounded by reporters from the trial

survive and probably won't." Like Faulkner, nearly all Americans who read newspapers, watched TV, or listened to the radio knew about the Emmett Till case, and the widespread press made many white Americans more supportive than ever of equal rights for African Americans.

Black Americans, of course, were already keenly aware of their second-class status in U.S. society, but before the Emmett Till case, no single event had ever generated enough support, enough publicity, or enough outrage to unify a large-scale effort to oppose segregation. The unification began when *Jet* magazine published its article about Emmett's murder along with the photo of Emmett in his casket. John H. Johnson, publisher of the magazine, recalled the impact it had on black readers: "The issue [of *Jet*], which went out on sale on September 15, 1955, sold out immediately and did as much as any other event to traumatize Black America and prepare the way for the Freedom Movement of the sixties."

Many young African Americans were traumatized by the story. In her memoir, *Coming of Age in Mississippi,* Anne Moody, who was fourteen when Emmett was murdered, explained that whatever innocence she might have had about being black in Mississippi vanished when she heard about the crime. She wrote, "Before Emmett Till's murder, I had known the fear of hunger, hell, and the Devil. But now there was a new fear known to me—the fear of being killed just because I was Black. This was the worst of my fears. I knew once I got food, the fear of starving to death would leave. I was also told that if I were a good girl, I wouldn't have to fear the Devil or hell. But I didn't know what one had to do or not do as a Negro not to be killed. Probably just being a Negro period was enough, I thought." Many others felt the same way, and their fear—and outrage at having to be afraid—inspired them to mobilize against racism.

Joyce Ladner was a young woman when Emmett was murdered, and her reaction to his death eventually led to her involvement in the civil rights movement, where she met many other young African American women who had also been motivated by the case. In a Brookings National Issues Forum in 2000, Ladner discussed the effects the *Jet* magazine photo and the news of the trial had on her and others. "When I met people like Judy [Richardson] and SNCC [Student Nonviolent Coordinating Committee] in 1962, '63, all of us remembered the photograph of Emmett Till's face, lying in the coffin, [in] *Jet* magazine. . . . Almost to a person, every one of my SNCC friends I've known 40 years can recall that photograph. . . . That galvanized a generation as a symbol—that was our symbol—that if they did it to him, they could do it to us."

The nationwide fallout from the Emmett Till case brought together politicians, NAACP workers, civil rights activists, church leaders, and ordinary black and white citizens. The senseless murder of the boy from Chicago was the last straw for all people opposed to racism. They knew that if they were ever to have freedom in their own land, they would have to take action soon. They knew that if they wanted to put an end to senseless murders, lynchings, and intimidation, they would have to make a stand. They knew that if they wanted to provide better lives for their children, they would have to put an end to discrimination, prejudice, and hatred. The trial of Emmett's killers was the necessary and final catalyst for a united effort against racial discrimination in America.

Rosa Parks, a forty-two-year-old seamstress from Montgomery, Alabama, was among those horrified and inspired by Emmett's murder. The ugliness of racism was nothing new to this lifelong resident of the Deep South—she had worked with the NAACP for some time—but the brutal murder of a child tore her heart. Parks's biographer, Douglas Brinkley, wrote that she cried when she saw the awful *Jet* magazine photo and that "the sight of it made her physically ill. . . . With the murder of Emmett Till, a new era of defiance in the name of civil rights was at hand."

Rosa Parks riding a city bus in 1956, after the Montgomery bus boycott

The Emmett Till case was not the sole cause of the civil rights movement, but it was the final indignity that caused the flood of outrage to overflow the dam of racial injustice. Brinkley points out that Rosa Parks did not plan to initiate a bus boycott on December 1, 1955, but her own weariness from a lifetime of discrimination made her determined not to surrender her seat to a white person on a Montgomery city bus that evening. "A lifetime's education in injustice—" wrote Brinkley, "from her grandfather's nightly vigils to the murder of Emmett Till—had strengthened her resolve to act when the time came." Parks's refusal to abide by the segregated busing laws in Montgomery led to the 381-day boycott of the city bus system, a boycott that brought Reverend Martin Luther King Jr. to prominence, brought an end to segregated public transportation in Alabama, and marked the first nationally publicized action in the modern civil rights movement. Parks would later write an endorsement of Mamie Till Bradley's memoir, crediting her involvement in the civil rights movement to Mrs. Bradley's decision to open Emmett's casket. "I am so thankful for the bravery and courage Mamie demonstrated when she shared her only child with the world. The news of Emmett's death caused many people to participate in the cry for justice and equal rights, including myself."

While progress was being made in the civil rights movement, the final threads of the Emmett Till case were unraveling. After their trial in September, Roy Bryant and J. W. Milam were sent back to jail to await a Leflore County grand jury's decision on their kidnapping charges. Even though both men had confessed to kidnapping Emmett, in November, the grand jury refused to indict them for the crime, and they were set free.

The life Bryant and Milam returned to in the Delta after the trial had changed. Even though many whites considered them heroes, black residents knew them to be cold-blooded killers and boycotted Bryant's store in Money and the other local businesses owned by Milam. Finances became tight for the two men and their families, and they had difficulty securing loans to keep their businesses afloat. Owing perhaps to their desperate need for money and to their racist arrogance, in December 1955, the two half brothers agreed to sell their story to *Look* magazine reporter William Bradford Huie. For $4,000, they granted Huie a series of interviews in the presence of their lawyers, and in those interviews they described why and how they murdered Emmett Till. Because they had already been acquitted of the crime, Bryant and Milam knew they could not be retried for the murder, no matter what details they might confess. They were careful, however, not to implicate anyone else in their story.

J. W. Milam and Roy Bryant leave the Leflore County courthouse in Greenwood, Mississippi, after posting bail for their kidnapping charges

The report of that interview, "The Shocking Story of Approved Killing in Mississippi," the last media blast of the Emmett Till case, appeared in the January 24, 1956, issue of *Look* magazine. The sensational article was reprinted in *Reader's Digest*, and a more detailed version of it appeared in Huie's book *Wolf Whistle and Other Stories* in 1959.

Milam told Huie that the brothers' original intention was to "just whip him . . . and scare some sense into him." After kidnapping

Emmett, they drove the dusty back roads of the Delta looking for a good place to beat and intimidate the boy, but their plan, according to Milam, didn't work. "We never were able to scare him. They [Northern rabble-rousers] had just filled him so full of that poison that he was hopeless." By then it was dawn, and the men drove to Leslie Milam's plantation and dragged Emmett into a shed, where they pistol-whipped his face and head. Throughout the beating, said the killers, Emmett remained defiant.

"Well, what could we do?" Milam asked Huie. "He was hopeless. . . . I just decided it was time a few people got put on notice. . . ." Milam continued, suggesting that a black man who even insinuated sex with a white woman was "tired o' livin'. I'm likely to kill him. . . . 'Chicago boy,' I said, 'I'm tired of 'em sending your kind down here to stir up trouble. Goddamn you, I'm going to make an example of you—just so everybody can know how me and my folks stand.' "

The two men told Huie how they made Emmett load a seventy-four-pound cotton gin fan into the back of their pickup. Then they forced Emmett to get into the truck, and they drove him to a secluded spot on the Tallahatchie River. It was a little after 7:00 Sunday morning when they pulled to a stop on the banks of the river. Bryant and Milam ordered Emmett to get out of the truck and strip off his clothes. According to the killers' story, he obeyed and stood, naked, before the two white men.

At gunpoint, Milam challenged the boy. "You still as good as I am?"

Milam said Emmett's answer was "Yeah."

"You've still 'had' white women?"

"Yeah," said Emmett.

That was all the enraged Milam needed to hear. He squeezed the trigger of his .45 pistol and fired an expanding bullet into Emmett's skull, killing him instantly. Then, according to their interview, they used barbed wire to tie the cotton gin fan around Emmett's neck and threw him into the muddy green water of the river.

Bryant and Milam's bold national confession in *Look* drew responses from all over the country. Most African Americans and whites were furious with the two men, but one letter to the editor of *Look* revealed that even after all that had happened in the months following the trial, racial intolerance still thrived in the hearts of some Americans. After criticizing the magazine for publishing the interview, the racist letter writer said, "Roy Bryant and J. W. Milam did what had to be done and their courage in taking the course they did is to be commended. To have followed any other course would have been unrealistic, cowardly and not in the best interests of their family or country."

Fortunately, that kind of attitude was in the minority. Most Southern whites, including those who had defended Bryant and Milam, shared the opinion of Will Campbell, the director of religious life at the University of Mississippi. In an interview, he said that those two men, who had once been considered heroes by many of their white neighbors, "were nobodies after that. They were disgraced. Which is a strange dichotomy in Southern society, that while they were being accused of this crime, we have to rally to their defense and take up money and hire lawyers and all the rest. But then when it's over, 'Look, why did you have to disgrace us like that? Now get out of town, we really don't want to see you again.'" Their chilling admission to the murder of a boy caused them to be ostracized by their community, and within a few years, both Bryant and Milam would leave Mississippi.

The *Look* magazine interview had an unintended effect on African

Americans. In addition to proving, beyond a doubt, that Bryant and Milam had kidnapped and murdered Emmett Till, it solidified their commitment to the fight for civil rights. If society had degenerated to the point where white men could murder an African American boy and then brag about it in a national magazine, something had to be done. In a television interview thirty years after the trial, African American historian Tim Black emphasized the impact of the *Look* article: "When [Bryant and Milam] made that story public of how they brutalized this boy because he would not say he was afraid of them as white people, that just turned us all on; it gave us new energy to get into it, so it was a stimulant, a major stimulant, in pushing people further and deeper into the civil rights movement." By then, January 1955, there was no turning back. Rosa Parks had started the Montgomery bus boycott, Martin Luther King Jr. had emerged as a powerful and charismatic leader of the new civil rights movement, and African Americans nationwide were committed to doing whatever they could to make equality the law of the land.

In the years that followed the *Look* article, Roy Bryant and J. W. Milam lived the rest of their lives in shame and anonymity. Their wives divorced them, and the two half brothers never regained their reputations or livelihoods in Mississippi. And, perhaps not surprisingly, both men remained unrepentant to the end of their lives. In a later interview with Huie, Milam said that even though the murder of Emmett Till had caused him lots of problems, he didn't regret the killing. In 1993, a resentful Roy Bryant told Plater Robinson that he was tired of hearing about the Emmett Till story. "Let that goddamn stuff die," he snapped when the reporter asked about Emmett. "Look what they're doing with Beckwith* down there now . . . And now they want to get me, so the hell with 'em. . . . Lot of people made a lot of money out of it; I ain't made a damn nickel."

Milam died in 1980, Bryant in 1994.

* Byron de la Beckwith was the Mississippi white supremacist who murdered Medgar Evers in 1963. A Mississippi court finally convicted him of the crime in 1994.

From left to right: Walter Billingsley, Willie Reed, Amanda Bradley, and Add Reed wait in the witness room

The courageous African Americans who testified against Milam and Bryant had to leave Mississippi soon after the trial. Willie Reed and his family moved to Chicago. Mose Wright accepted a job in Albany, New York, and gave away Dallas, "the best dog in seven states," and abandoned his car at a train depot before saying good-bye to Mississippi forever.

Mamie Till Bradley continued to travel the country giving lectures about her son and the civil rights movement and advocating for racial equality and harmony. In 1956, she enrolled in Chicago Teachers College to complete her

Emmett Till's mother stands in front of a portrait of her son on the fortieth anniversary of his murder in 1955

teaching degree; four years later she began a long, satisfying career as an elementary school teacher in Chicago. But Mrs. Bradley would never be able to return to the kind of life she had enjoyed before her son's death. Her life and the lives of millions of Americans were permanently changed on a hot August night in 1955. The murder of Emmett Till taught America about the urgent need for equal rights for all citizens, regardless of race, but Emmett's mother learned perhaps the most painful and longest-lasting lesson of all. In a newspaper interview a month after the conclusion of the trial in Sumner, she told reporters, "Two months ago I had a nice apartment in Chicago. I had a good job. I had a son. When something happened to the Negroes in the South, I said, 'That's their business, not mine.' Now I know how wrong I was. The murder of my son has shown me that what happens to any of us, anywhere in the world, had better be the business of us all."

It still is the business of us all.

CHAPTER 8

THE CASE IN THE TWENTY-FIRST CENTURY

Sunday, July 23, 2012, Sanford, Florida, about forty miles west of the Atlantic coast

The sun had just dipped below the horizon when seventeen-year-old Trayvon Martin left a local convenience store, a cold can of Arizona iced tea and a bag of Skittles in his pockets. He tugged the hood of his gray sweatshirt over his head as he walked through a cluster of townhouses where he was staying with a family friend.

Sitting in an SUV parked along a curb in the gated Twin Lakes community, twenty-eight-year-old George Zimmerman, the neighborhood watch coordinator, noticed a black kid in a hoodie walking through the complex—and didn't like what he saw. After watching Trayvon for a few minutes, Zimmerman called the police to report "a real suspicious guy" walking through the property, a black kid who "looks like he's up to no good." Minutes later, Zimmerman said that the teen had started running. "These assholes," he muttered as he got out of his SUV, "they always get away."

"Are you following him?" asked the dispatcher.

"Yeah," Zimmerman replied.

"Okay, we don't need you to do that." The dispatcher ended the call by telling Zimmerman that police were on their way.

That's when things fell apart.

After trailing Trayvon for a few minutes, Zimmerman caught up with him, and they exchanged words briefly before a fight started. At some point, Zimmerman pulled out his 9mm pistol and fired a single shot that pierced Trayvon's heart.

Police arrived seconds later to find Trayvon facedown in the grass. He had no pulse. Responders attempted CPR, but the boy was dead.

News of the teenager's death spread quickly and provoked powerful and polarizing reactions. Some defended Zimmerman's right to "stand his ground" and protect himself with deadly force. Others accused Zimmerman of racial profiling and murder. Zimmerman claimed that Trayvon had started the fight and would have killed him if he hadn't had a gun. Many people mourned the death of a teenage boy apparently murdered for doing nothing more than walking home on a Sunday evening.

In the weeks and months that followed, a media frenzy surrounded the killing. Witnesses, police, lawyers, and family members connected to the case were all interviewed. Zimmerman admitted shooting Trayvon, but he maintained it was in self-defense, and his lawyers cited a Florida law that allows citizens to use deadly force when under attack. Trayvon's family and civil rights groups argued that Trayvon had done nothing wrong and that his death was racially motivated.

Protesters in Stanford, Florida, march in support of Trayvon Martin on March 31, 2012

It wasn't long before people drew parallels between Trayvon Martin's death and the murder of another black teenager fifty-seven years earlier: Emmett Till. The reference to one of the most famous victims of racist violence in American history showed that despite the election of an African American president in 2008, the United States had yet to achieve the dream of racial equality and tolerance hoped for by Martin Luther King Jr. and other civil rights activists.

As with the Emmett Till case, various media sources portrayed both the victim and the perpetrator as good guys or bad guys: Trayvon was a decent kid, a typical high school student—or a drug-using gang banger. Zimmerman was a dedicated, community-minded hero—or a racist bully. Tension in the case escalated when the district attorney charged Zimmerman with second-degree murder and ordered him to stand trial in June 2013. The governor of Florida appointed a special prosecutor to handle the case, and many Americans hoped justice would be done, hoped that our country had made progress since the trial of Emmett Till's murderers in 1955. Zimmerman's trial, which received intense media attention, lasted three weeks, and after the closing arguments, the six-woman jury deliberated sixteen hours before declaring George Zimmerman not guilty.

The acquittal sparked weeks of outrage, vigils, and protests and inspired the protest cry "Black lives matter!" which led to a major social justice movement. Days after the trial concluded, President Barack Obama held a White House press conference to respond to the verdict. After discussing the case and his personal experience with the complexity of race in America, he said "It's going to be important for all of us to do some soul searching." Since then, that soul searching has deepened, and the deaths of other young African Americans, including Jordan Davis, Michael Brown, and Tamir Rice, has continued to propel the Black Lives Matter movement.

And each death triggered recollections of the Emmett Till case.

Before 2003, except for two academic books on the case, the story of Emmett Till had been largely overlooked, buried for decades. Its reemergence began with the release of Stanley Nelson's PBS documentary, *The Murder of Emmett Till* in 2003. The film premiered at the Sundance Film Festival before its nationwide television broadcast on Martin Luther King Day, and it helped revive interest in the case. This book, *Getting Away with Murder: The True Story of the Emmett Till Case,* and an academic book, *The Murder of Emmett Till: A Documentary Narrative,* appeared a few months later, and the floodgates opened. Over the next fifteen years, newspaper and magazine articles; music, paintings, poems, and photographs; books and films about Emmett Till helped keep his story alive.

Emmett's mother, Mamie Till Mobley (she remarried in 1957), died shortly before the PBS documentary aired, and ten months later, her memoir, *Death of Innocence: The Story of the Hate Crime that Changed America,* was published. The book shared memories of her son, not as a civil rights martyr, but as a regular kid growing up in Chicago. In 2005, Keith Beauchamp's documentary, *The Untold Story of Emmett Louis Till,* uncovered new information, including interviews with witnesses who had never before spoken publicly about the case. As part of the pre-release work on the film, Beauchamp and his supporters, led by Alvin Sykes, lobbied federal authorities to reopen the case. They believed it would be possible to prosecute some of the previously unindicted people who had been involved in the murder. Emmett's mother knew about and supported these efforts. In her memoir, she wrote, "For years, I have hoped to have the investigation of the murder of my son reopened. . . . I have said repeatedly that I was determined to work until my dying

Civil rights activist Alvin Sykes worked tirelessly to persuade federal authorities to reopen the Emmett Till murder case

day to search for answers and to make sure that the story of Emmett Louis Till would never be buried."

Beauchamp's efforts worked, and in May 2004, the U.S. Justice Department announced its decision to reopen the case and to turn the new investigation over to the FBI. Under the direction of special agent Dale Killinger, the FBI conducted an aggressive eighteen-month investigation that involved searching for evidence, finding and interviewing witnesses, and conducting forensic studies that didn't exist in the 1950s, all of which resulted in a report of about eight thousand pages.

The findings were both encouraging and disappointing.

For decades, historians and family members had wondered how many men had been involved in Emmett's murder, how Emmett had died, and what evidence may have been overlooked. Many of those questions were finally answered by the investigation. Though Roy Bryant and J. W. Milam had, in 1956, claimed to have acted alone in the kidnapping and murder, extensive interviews by the FBI confirmed that at least three additional white men—Leslie Milam, Melvin Campbell, and one who has not been conclusively identified—were in the shed when Emmett was tortured and murdered. However, all three men were dead when the new investigation began, so this discovery didn't lead to any new indictments. Investigators also uncovered important artifacts that officials and historians had believed were lost years ago. One informant led agents to the murder weapon, the .45 pistol used to shoot Emmett. Additional information helped agents recover a copy of the original trial transcripts, a priceless document thought to have been destroyed in the 1960s. But there would be even more evidence to come.

Hoping to discover additional forensic evidence that could help the prosecution, the FBI requested and received permission to exhume Emmett's body from

On June 1, 2005, the FBI exhumed Emmett Till's body from its resting place in Burr Oak Cemetery in Alsip, Illinois

its grave in Burr Oak Cemetery in Alsip, Illinois, a small town about forty-five minutes southwest of Chicago.

On the morning of June 1, 2005, family members and close friends gathered for a brief prayer service inside a white tent that had been raised over Emmett's burial site. When the meeting concluded, FBI agents and police joined family members to watch as a backhoe started digging. Within a few hours, a white flatbed crane truck moved into position, lifted the concrete vault that contained Emmett's casket from its grave, and lowered it onto the flatbed. The FBI Evidence Response Team and other workers strapped the casket down and covered it with a pale blue plywood container that would protect it on the twenty-mile drive to a forensic lab in Chicago.

Examiners found that Emmett's body was remarkably well preserved, allowing them to conduct successful DNA tests and an autopsy. To almost no one's surprise, a tissue sample confirmed Emmett's identity and exposed as a lie Bryant and Milam's claim that the body pulled from the Tallahatchie River in 1955 was not Emmett Till. The autopsy and CT scan yielded more sobering information: Emmett had not only been shot, as Bryant and Milam had admitted in 1956, but he had also endured horrendous torture that fractured his skull, crushed his throat, and broke both his wrists and his left thigh. Unfortunately, the autopsy and forensic study did not turn up evidence strong enough to convict any of the additional suspects who may have been involved in the crime.

The agents assigned to the case worked long hours to complete the lengthy final report, which was then sent to Washington, DC, to be reviewed and approved by both FBI officials and by the Justice Department. After the full report was approved in March 2006, it was delivered to Joyce Chiles, the first African American district attorney to serve the Mississippi counties where Emmett's murder had taken place. Chiles had been born in a small Mississippi town near Money just a few months before Emmett Till died. Though born, raised, and educated in Mississippi, Chiles hadn't heard much about the Till murder case until a junior high classmate showed her the famous photo of Emmett in his casket.

As the newly elected district attorney, Chiles welcomed the opportunity to review the FBI report, but she was determined to maintain legal impartiality despite the deep significance of the case. It took nearly a year for her and her legal team to review the full file, but when they completed their review, which included a detailed briefing from Killinger, Chiles convened a grand jury to consider possible charges against Mississippi residents, including Carolyn Bryant, who may have been accessories to the murder. If the grand jury considered the evidence strong enough to win a conviction, they could issue indictments leading to a new trial, and many people throughout the United States hoped desperately that indictments would come. After hearing evidence for two days, however, the grand jury determined that the material was not compelling enough to warrant any indictments, and their decision closed the book on the Emmett Till case.

Fortunately, though, their decision didn't end the legacy of Emmett Till. The FBI investigation rekindled public interest in the case, which has resulted in a number of initiatives that have kept the story alive.

One such initiative came from a determination not only to remember Emmett Till but also to work to resolve other cold cases, especially racist crimes that were never prosecuted. In 2007, thanks to persistent lobbying by Alvin Sykes, civil rights activist and Congressional Representative John Lewis of Georgia introduced legislation that would fund investigations into other unsolved civil rights cases. Many Americans, especially Emmett's extended family, applauded the Till Bill, officially titled the "Emmett Till Unsolved Civil Rights Crimes Act," which was signed by President George W. Bush on October 7, 2008. President Barack Obama continued the legacy of that legislation on December 16, 2016, when he signed a re-authorization of the bill that extended its scope "to include the investigation and prosecution of criminal civil rights statutes violations that occurred before 1980 and resulted in a death."

Emmett Till's family members viewed this legislation as vindication of their long—and sometimes futile—efforts to have justice served in the Emmett Till case. In his 2010 memoir, *Simeon's Story: An Eyewitness Account of the Kidnapping of Emmett Till,* Simeon Wright, son of Mose Wright and cousin of Emmett Till, praised Congress' action: "Of all the memorials, monuments, and other commemorations of Bobo's life, nothing pleases me more than to have this bill in tribute to his very brief stay among us, a short life in which he was made a martyr long before he had a chance to live up to his potential." Wright's memoir provided important new perspectives on the case, including memories of Emmett and the kidnapping (Wright had shared a bedroom with Emmett the night he was abducted) and countered some of the misinformation about the case that had circulated for decades, including the details of what happened at Bryants' store and what his father had said in court.

Since 2004, Wright and his nephew Wheeler Parker, who was also in the house the night of the kidnapping, have traveled the country speaking to students about the case and the importance of remembering Emmett Till's legacy. Parker often reminds students that despite the trauma he and his family suffered because of Emmett's murder, he is not driven by revenge or hatred. Rather he sees talking about the case as an opportunity for healing and understanding. Parker believes that "Hate hurts the hater," so he encourages his audiences, "Don't hate, appreciate."

Interviews with Wright, Parker, Mamie Till Mobley, and others connected to the case, combined with the new information from the FBI investigation, led to the creation of a major new work. In 2015, the University Press of Mississippi published Devery Anderson's *Emmett Till: The Murder that Shocked the World and Propelled the Civil Rights Movement,* a book that has been praised as the single most important work about the case. More than a decade in the making, Anderson's 552 pages cover, in richly researched and well-documented detail, every aspect of the case and of the people involved—including the circumstances related to the execution of Emmett's father and how Bryant and

Milam's defense team tried to use that information to make a like-father, like-son argument that Emmett was predisposed to criminal behavior.

After Anderson's book, it seemed as if there was nothing left to be said about the Emmett Till case, but in 2017, Timothy Tyson delivered some headline-grabbing new information. His book *The Blood of Emmett Till* covers much of the same territory as Anderson's, but it drew national and international attention for its account of an interview between Tyson and Carolyn Bryant, the woman who had accused Emmett of assaulting her. Bryant had been interviewed by Killinger and the FBI in 2004, but she told essentially the same story she had given in court in 1955. Her discussion with the FBI, however, changed her heart, and in 2005, she contacted Tyson because she admired a book, *Blood Done Sign My Name,* he had published a year earlier. She invited him to her home and for the first time spoke openly about her role in the case. She told Tyson that, after fifty years, there were some details she simply couldn't remember, but she did remember—and admitted to—lying in her courtroom testimony. Her husband, his family, and his lawyers had pressured her to say that Emmett had grabbed her in the store and said "unprintable," sexual things to her. "That part's not true," she confessed to Tyson. "Nothing that boy did could ever justify what happened to him."

In addition to Anderson's and Tyson's books, several new movie projects will likely go a long way toward establishing Emmett Till's story as a more prominent thread in the fabric of American history. At least four films are now in various stages of development, each based on previously published work about the case: Jay Z and Will Smith plan a six-part HBO series using Devery Anderson's book; Whoopi Goldberg and Keith Beauchamp are developing a feature film based on Simeon Wright's memoir; Chaz Ebert is working on a biopic of Mamie Till Mobley based on her memoir; and David Barr III and David Scott Hay are adapting a play script written by Mamie Till Mobley. It's impossible to predict the success or impact of these films, but the attention filmmakers have given to the Emmett Till case shows how his story is, unfortunately, still relevant in today's society. This time around, however, mainstream America is paying better attention.

The opening of the Smithsonian's National Museum of African American History and Culture in September 2016 marked a significant milestone in recognizing the importance of African Americans in the history of the United States. One section on the lower level of the museum contains an exhibit about the Emmett Till case. When he was re-buried after the FBI investigation, he was placed in a new casket, and the original casket was stored in a warehouse on the cemetery property. As the Smithsonian was gathering artifacts for its new museum, Lonnie Bunch, the director, acquired the casket for part of an exhibition about the case. The decision to create the exhibit was a difficult one. "Was that too ghoulish?" Bunch wondered before going on to explain, "I never wanted to exoticize or exploit Emmett's murder, but I kept hearing his mother's voice as she used to always talk to me about how important it was to her that Emmett didn't die in vain." Exhibit space in one of America's most famous museums will sustain the legacy of Emmett Till.

The Smithsonian's National Museum of African American History and Culture is home to Emmett Till's original casket

Back in 1958, Martin Luther King Jr. understood the importance of remembering the tragedy and impact of the Emmett Till case, and he seemed to know that racist violence hadn't ended. "Today it is Emmett Till," he told a mass meeting at Beulah Baptist Church in Montgomery, "tomorrow it is Martin Luther King. Then in another tomorrow it will be somebody else." Trayvon Martin is only one of those "somebody else," but his death and the rise of the Black Lives Matter movement are reminders that our nation has yet to fully realize the promise of the Fourteenth Amendment that all citizens are entitled to "equal protection of the laws."

If we have learned anything in the twenty-first century from the Emmett Till case, it's that our fellow citizens—and our common history—matter. Progress is possible, and our understanding of civil rights history is essential in that progress. In his eulogy for Clementa Pinckney, pastor of the Emanuel African Methodist Episcopal Church in Charleston, South Carolina, who in 2016 was murdered in a racist massacre, President Barack Obama reminded us, "history can't be a sword to justify injustice or a shield against progress. It must be a manual for how to avoid repeating the mistakes of the past, how to break the cycle, a roadway toward a better world."

That roadway lies ahead of us.

Time Line

U.S. Civil Rights Events, Including the Details of the Emmett Till Case

September 18, 1850	Fugitive Slave Act
March 6, 1857	Supreme Court Decision, *Dred Scott v. John F. A. Sanford*
April 12, 1861	Fort Sumter fired on by Confederate forces
January 1, 1863	President Lincoln issues the Emancipation Proclamation
April 9, 1865	General Robert E. Lee surrenders to Ulysses S. Grant at Appomattox
December 1865	Ku Klux Klan organized
June 13, 1866	Fourteenth Amendment (citizenship)
February 26, 1869	Fifteenth Amendment (voting)
March 1, 1875	Civil Rights Act of 1875
May 18, 1896	Supreme Court Decision, *Plessy v. Ferguson* (doctrine of "separate but equal")
February 12, 1909	NAACP organized
April 1931 to July 1937	Trials of the Scottsboro Boys
August 1936	Four African American athletes, Jesse Owens, Cornelius Johnson, Archie Williams, and John Woodruff, win six individual gold medals at the Berlin Olympics
June 25, 1941	President Roosevelt issues Executive Order 8802, banning racial discrimination in the defense industry
July 24, 1941	**Emmett Louis Till born**
April 15, 1947	Jackie Robinson becomes the first African American to play in the modern major leagues
May 17, 1954	Supreme Court Decision, *Brown v. Topeka Board of Education*
July 11, 1954	White Citizens' Council founded
May 7, 1955	Rev. George Lee, Mississippi voter registration activist, murdered
May 31, 1955	Supreme Court issues implementation order: school integration must commence"with all deliberate speed"
August 13, 1955	Lamar Smith, Mississippi voter registration activist, murdered
August 21, 1955	**Emmett Till arrives in Mississippi**
August 24, 1955	**Incident at Bryant's Grocery & Meat Market**
August 28, 1955	**Emmett Till kidnapped and murdered**
August 29, 1955	**J. W. Milam and Roy Bryant arrested for kidnapping Emmett Till**
August 31, 1955	**Emmett Till's body found in the Tallahatchie River**
September 3–6, 1955	**Open-casket viewing in Chicago**
September 6, 1955	**Emmett's funeral in Chicago**
September 6, 1955	**Grand jury indicts Milam and Bryant on kidnapping and murder charges**
September 9, 1955	**Trial date set**

September 15, 1955	***Jet* magazine publishes photo of Emmett Till's mutilated corpse**
September 19, 1955	**Trial begins in Sumner, Mississippi**
September 21, 1955	**Mose Wright testifies; identifies Milam and Bryant as kidnappers**
September 22, 1955	**Emmett's mother testifies**
September 23, 1955	**Jury finds Milam and Bryant not guilty**
December 1, 1955	Rosa Parks refuses to give up her seat on a Montgomery bus
December 5, 1955	Montgomery Bus Boycott begins
January 24, 1956	***Look* magazine publishes a confession/interview with Milam and Bryant**
August 29, 1957	Civil Rights Act of 1957
September 23, 1957	Nine African American students integrate Central High School in Little Rock, Arkansas
May 6, 1960	Civil Rights Act of 1960
November 14, 1960	First grader Ruby Bridges, accompanied by U.S. marshals, integrates an elementary school in New Orleans
September 30, 1962	Riots at the University of Mississippi protesting the enrollment of James Meredith, an African American student
June 12, 1963	Civil rights activist Medgar Evers murdered in Jackson, Mississippi
August 28, 1963	Martin Luther King Jr.'s "I Have a Dream" Speech
September 15, 1963	Four girls, Addie Mae Collins (14), Carol Denise McNair (11), Carole Robertson (14), and Cynthia Wesley (14), killed in the bombing of the 16th Street Baptist Church in Birmingham, Alabama
June 1964	"Freedom Summer," voter registration project in Mississippi
June 21, 1964	Three civil rights workers, James Chaney, Andrew Goodman, and Michael Schwerner, murdered in Mississippi
July 2, 1964	Civil Rights Act of 1964
March 7, 1965	"Bloody Sunday," march to Selma, Alabama
August 6, 1965	Voting Rights Act of 1965
April 4, 1968	Martin Luther King, Jr. murdered in Memphis, Tennessee
April 11, 1968	Civil Rights Act of 1968

The Emmett Till Case in the 21st Century

January 6, 2003	Emmett's mother, Mamie Till Mobley, dies
January 19, 2003	PBS documentary, *The Murder of Emmett Till*, airs nationwide
January–December 2004	Documentarian Keith Beauchamp begins private screenings of *The Untold Story of Emmett Louis Till* and starts a petition campaign to reopen the case
April 11, 2004	Artist Franklin McMahon donates his courtroom drawings from *Life* magazine to the Chicago Historical Society
May 10, 2004	U.S. Justice Department announces the case is reopened; FBI investigation begins
October 24, 2004	*60 Minutes* feature on the case
May 4, 2005	Exhumation and autopsy of Emmett Till announced
May 18, 2005	Copy of trial transcripts discovered
August 28, 2005	Fiftieth anniversary of the kidnapping of Emmett Till
October 24, 2005	Rosa Parks dies
March 16, 2006	FBI announces that no federal charges will be filed

February 11, 2007	Mississippi schedules a Leflore County grand jury to review evidence against Carolyn Bryant
February 27, 2007	Leflore County grand jury declines to indict Carolyn Bryant or anyone else
March 30, 2007	FBI releases results of investigation, including trial transcripts, online
August 28, 2009	Emmett Till's casket to be displayed in the new Smithsonian Museum of African American History and Culture
January 14, 2014	Juanita Milam, wife of J. W. Milam, dies
August 19, 2015	*Emmett Till: The Murder That Shocked the World and Propelled the Civil Rights Movement,* Devery Anderson's comprehensive account of the case, published
January 31, 2017	*The Blood of Emmett Till*, Timothy B. Tyson's book, includes an unprecedented interview with Carolyn Bryant

Bibliography

Anderson, Devery. *Emmett Till: The Murder that Shocked the World and Propelled the Civil Rights Movement.* Oxford, MS: UP of Mississippi, 2015.

Bergman, Peter M., et al. *The Chronological History of the Negro in America.* New York: Harper and Row, 1969.

Brady, Tom P. *Black Monday*. Winona, Mississippi: Association of Citizens' Councils, 1955.

Brinkley, Douglas. *Rosa Parks*. New York: Viking/Penguin Putnam, 2000.

Carson, Clayborne, et al, eds. *The Eyes on the Prize Civil Rights Reader*. New York: Penguin, 1991.

David Halberstam's The Fifties. "Episode 6: The Rage Within." Dir. Alex Gibney and Tracy Dahlby. Videocassette. The History Channel, 1997.

Davis, Townsend. *Weary Feet, Rested Souls: A Guided History of the Civil Rights Movement*. New York: W. W. Norton and Company, 1998.

"Death in Mississippi." *The Commonweal*, 62 (September 23, 1955): 603–604.

Durham, Michael S. *Powerful Days: The Civil Rights Photography of Charles Moore*. New York: Stewart, Tabori, and Chang, 1991.

Ebony Pictorial History of Black America, vols. 2 and 3. Nashville: The Southwestern Company, 1971.

Evers-Williams, Myrlie with Williams Peters. *For Us, the Living*. Jackson, Mississippi: Banner Books, 1967, 1996.

Eyes on the Prize: "Awakenings (1954–56)." Dir. Henry Hampton. Videocassette. Blackside, 1987.

Faulkner, William. *Essays, Speeches, and Public Letters*. New York: Random House, 1965.

Friedman, Leon, ed. *The Civil Rights Reader: Basic Documents of the Civil Rights Movement.* New York: Walker and Company, 1967.

Goldsby, Jacqueline. "The High and Low Tech of It: The Meaning of Lynching and the Death of Emmett Till." *The Yale Journal of Criticism* (9.2) 1966: 245–282.

Halberstam, David. *The Fifties.* New York: Villard, 1993.

Hampton, Henry, et al, eds. *Voices of Freedom: An Oral History of the Civil Rights Movement from the 1950s through the 1980s*. New York: Bantam, 1990.

Hendrickson, Paul. "Mississippi Haunting." *The Washington Post.* February 27, 2000 (Proquest).

Horton, James Oliver and Lois E. Horton, eds. *A History of the African American People*. Detroit: Wayne State UP, 1997.

Hudson-Weems, Clenora. *Emmett Till: The Sacrificial Lamb of the Civil Rights Movement*. Troy, Michigan: Bedford Publishers, 1994.

Huie, William Bradford. "The Shocking Story of Approved Killing in Mississippi." *Look*. January 24, 1956: 46–50.

———. "What's Happened to the Emmett Till Killers?" *Look* 21 (January 22, 1957): 63–66, 68.

———. *Wolf Whistle and Other Stories*. New York: Signet, 1959.

Hurley, F. Jack, et al. *Pictures Tell the Story: Ernest C. Withers Reflections in History*. Norfolk, Virginia: Chrysler Museum of Art, 2000.

"In Memoriam, Emmett Till." *Life*. (39) October 10, 1955: 48.

Kasher, Steven. *The Civil Rights Movement: Photographic History, 1954–1968*. New York: Abbeville Press, 1996.

Kosof, Anna. *The Civil Rights Movement and Its Legacy*. New York: Franklin Watts, 1989.

Larsson, Clotye Murdock. "Land of the Till Murder Revisited." *Ebony*. 41 (March 1986): 53–54, 56–58.

Long, Richard A. *Black Americana*. Secaucus, NJ: Chartwell Books, 1986.

Lyon, Danny. *Memories of the Southern Civil Rights Movement*. Chapel Hill: University of North Carolina Press, 1992.

"M is for Mississippi and Murder." New York, New York: NAACP, 1955.

Moody, Anne. *Coming of Age in Mississippi.* New York: Dial, 1968.

Muse, Benjamin. *Ten Years of Prelude: The Story of Integration Since the Supreme Court's 1954 Decision.* New York: Viking, 1964.

Myers, Walter Dean. *One More River to Cross: An African American Photograph Album.* New York: Harcourt Brace, 1995.

"Nation Horrified by Murder of Kidnaped Chicago Youth." *Jet,* 8 (September 15, 1955): 6-9.

Peavy, Charles D. *Go Slow Now: Faulkner and the Race Question.* Eugene, Oregon: University of Oregon Books, 1971.

Powledge, Fred. *We Shall Overcome: Heroes of the Civil Rights Movement.* New York: Charles Scribner's Sons, 1993.

"Race: The Great American Divide. Panel 1: We Shall Overcome: Recalling the Civil Rights Struggles of the '50s and '60s." Brookings National Issues Forum, January 11, 2000. http://www.brook.edu/comm/transcripts/20000111/panel1.htm, October 10, 2001.

Robinson, Armstead L. and Patricia Sullivan, eds. *New Directions in Civil Rights Studies*. Charlottesville, VA: UP of Virginia, 1991.

Robinson, Plater. "The Murder of Emmett Till." http://www.soundprint.org/documentaries/more_info/emmett_till.phtml

Shakoor, Jordana Y. *Civil Rights Childhood*. Jackson, Mississippi: UP of Mississippi, 1999.

Terkel, Studs. *Race: How Blacks and Whites Think and Feel about the American Obsession*. New York: The New Press, 1992.

Thompson, Kathleen and Hilary Mac Austin, eds. *The Face of Our Past: Images of Black Women from Colonial America to the Present*. Bloomington: Indiana UP, 1999.

Tolnay, Stewart E. and E. M. Beck. *A Festival of Violence: An Analysis of Southern Lynchings, 1882–1930.* Urbana: University of Illinois Press, 1995.

Twentieth-Century America: A Primary Source Collection from the Associated Press by the Writers and Photographers of the Associated Press. Danbury, Conn.: Grolier Educational Corp., 1995.

Tyson, Timothy B. *The Blood of Emmett Till.* New York: Simon & Schuster, 2017.

Wakefield, Dan. "Justice in Sumner: Land of the Free." *The Nation,* October 1, 1955.

———. *Revolt in the South.* New York: Grove Press, 1960.

Waldron, Ann. *Hodding Carter: The Reconstruction of a Racist*. Chapel Hill, North Carolina: Algonquin Books of Chapel Hill, 1993.

Wesley, John Milton. "The Final Days of Emmett Till: Legacy of a Lynching in Our Little Mississippi Town." http://www.cunepress.com/cunepress/booksonline/essays/etg/etg-pages/r-w/wesley.htm#essay.

Wexler, Sanford. *The Civil Rights Movement: An Eyewitness History*. New York: Facts on File, 1993.

Whitfield, Stephen J. *Death in the Delta*. Baltimore: Johns Hopkins UP, 1988.

Whittaker, Hugh Stephen. "A Case Study in Southern Justice: The Emmett Till Case." Master's Thesis, Florida State University, 1963.

Williams, Juan. *Eyes on the Prize: America's Civil Rights Years, 1954-1965* New York: Viking, 1987.

Additional Resources on the Emmett Till Case

Websites

"African-American History," http://afroamhistory.about.com/

"African American History Civil Rights Movement," http://www.academicinfo.net/africanamcr.html

"African American Odyssey," http://memory.loc.gov/ammem/aaohtml/exhibit/aointro.html

"Afro-American Almanac," http://www.toptags.com/aama/

"American Experience: The Murder of Emmett Till," http://www.pbs.org/wgbh/amex/till/

"Civil Rights History—U.S. Civil Rights Movement," http://www.academicinfo.net/africanamcr.html

"Civil Rights in Mississippi: A Digital Archive," http://www.lib.usm.edu/~spcol/crda/index.html

"Emmett Till Murder Scene," http://www.emmetttillmurder.com

"Eyes on the Prize: A Teaching Guide by Plater Robinson," http://www.tulane.edu/~so-inst/eyes.html

"Historic Places of the Civil Rights Movement," http://www.cr.nps.gov/nr/travel/civilrights/

"The History of Jim Crow," http://jimcrowhistory.org/

"The Murder of Emmett Till," http://soundprint.org/radio/display_show/ID/398/name/The+Murder+of+Emmett+Till

"National Civil Rights Museum Virtual Tour," http://www.mecca.org/~crights/cyber.html

"Remembering Jim Crow," http://www.americanradioworks.org/features/remembering/

"The Rise and Fall of Jim Crow," http://www.pbs.org/wnet/jimcrow/

"Teaching Tolerance," (Southern Poverty Law Center) http://www.tolerance.org/teach/index.jsp

Artistic Works Based on the Emmett Till Murder

Blues for Mr. Charlie, a play by James Baldwin, 1964

"A Bronzeville Mother Loiters in Mississippi. Meanwhile, A Mississippi Mother Burns Bacon," a poem by Gwendolyn Brooks, 1960

"The Death of Emmett Till," a folk song by Bob Dylan, 1963

Dreaming Emmett, a play by Toni Morrison, 1986

"Emmett Till," a poem by James A. Emanuel, 1968

The Guardian, a play by I'm Ready Productions Inc., 2000

"The Last Quatrain of the Ballad of Emmett Till," a poem by Gwendolyn Brooks

Mississippi and the Face of Emmett Till, a play by Mamie Till Mobley and David Barr

Mississippi Trial, 1955, a novel by Chris Crowe, 2002

"My Name is Emmett Till," a song by Emmy Lou Harris, 2011

Playhouse 90: "Noon on Doomsday," 1956 (Rod Serling)

Playhouse 90: "A Town Has Turned to Dust," 1958 (Rod Serling)

Playhouse 90: "The Monsters are Due on Maple Street," 1960 (Rod Serling)

Poem for Emmett Till, a work for solo cello by William Roper, 2001

The State of Mississippi vs. Emmett Till, a play by David Barr, 1999

This Unsafe Star, a play by Chris Maly, 2005

Wolf Whistle, a novel by Leslie Nordan, 1995

A Wreath for Emmett Till, linked sonnets by Marilyn Nelson, 2005

Your Blues Ain't Like Mine, a novel by Bebe Moore Campbell, 1992

Film Documentaries

David Halberstam's The Fifties. "Episode 6: The Rage Within." Dir. Alex Gibney and Tracy Dahlby. Videocassette. The History Channel, 1997.

Eyes on the Prize: "Awakenings (1954–56)." Dir. Henry Hampton. Videocassette. Blackside, 1987.

The Murder of Emmett Till. Dir. Stanley Nelson. DVD. PBS, 2003.

The Untold Story of Emmett Louis Till. Dir. Keith A. Beauchamp. DVD. Velocity/Thinkfilm, 2006.

For Further Reading

Anderson, Devery. *Emmett Till: The Murder that Shocked the World and Propelled the Civil Rights Movement.* Oxford, MS: UP of Mississippi, 2015.

Bolden, Tonya. *Tell All the Children Our Story: Memories and Mementoes of Being Young and Black in America.* New York: Henry A. Abrams, 2002.

Brinkley, Douglas. *Rosa Parks*. New York: Viking/Penguin Putnam, 2000.

Chafe, William Henry, et al, eds. *Remembering Jim Crow: African Americans Tell About Life in the Segregated South*. New York: The New Press, 2001.

Crowe, Chris. *Mississippi Trial, 1955.* New York: Phyllis Fogelman Books, 2002.

Houck, Davis W. and Matthew A. Grindy. *Emmett Till and the Mississippi Press.* Oxford, MS: UP of Mississippi, 2008.

Houck, Davis W., ed. "Special Issue: 50 Years Later: Emmett Till, Rosa Parks, and Martin Luther King, Jr." Rhetoric and Public Affairs 8.2 (Summer 2005).

Hudson-Weems, Clenora. *Emmett Till: The Sacrificial Lamb of the Civil Rights Movement.* Troy, Michigan: Bedford Publishers, 1994.

Kluger, Richard. *Simple Justice: The History of Brown v. Board of Education and Black America's Struggle for Equality*. New York: Knopf, 1976.

Levine, Ellen, ed. *Freedom's Children: Young Civil Rights Activists Tell Their Own Stories.* New York: G. P. Putnam, 1993.

Meltzer, Milton, ed. *The Black Americans: A History in their Own Words.* New York: Harper, 1984.

Metress, Christopher, ed. *The Lynching of Emmett Till: A Documentary Narrative.* Charlottesville, Virginia: University of Virginia Press, 2002.

Myers, Walter Dean. *One More River to Cross: An African American Photograph Album*. New York: Harcourt Brace, 1995.

Nelson, Marilyn. *A Wreath for Emmett Till.* Boston: Houghton Mifflin, 2005.

Pollack, Harriet and Christopher Metress, eds. *Emmett Till in Literary Memory and Imagination.* Baton Rouge, Louisiana State UP, 2008.

Robinson, Plater. "The Murder of Emmett Till." http://www.soundprint.org/documentaries/more_info/emmett_till.phtml

Till-Mobley, Mamie and Christopher Benson. Death of Innocence: *The Story of the Hate Crime That Changed America.* New York: Random House, 2003.

Tyson, Timothy, B. *The Blood of Emmett Till.* New York: Simon & Schuster, 2017.

Wexler, Sanford. *The Civil Rights Movement: An Eyewitness History.* New York: Facts on File, 1993.

Whitfield, Stephen J. *Death in the Delta.* Baltimore: Johns Hopkins UP, 1988.

Wideman, John Edgar. *Writing to Save a Life: The Louis Till Story.* New York: Scribner, 2016.

Williams, Juan. *Eyes on the Prize: America's Civil Rights Years, 1954–1965.* New York: Viking, 1987.

Wright, Simeon with Herb Boyd. *Simeon's Story: An Eyewitness Account of the Kidnapping of Emmett Till.* Chicago: Lawrence Hill Books, 2010.